Remember? Remember?

CHARLES BEAUMONT

Remember?

Remember?

THE MACMILLAN COMPANY, NEW YORK

The author is very grateful to Miss Mary Noel for allowing him to quote from pages 146–148 of her admirable book, *Villains Galore;* and to August Derleth for permission to quote from his remarks concerning a review of "pulp fiction."

© Charles Beaumont 1963
Seven chapters originally appeared, in somewhat different form, in *Playboy* Magazine (HMH Publishing Co., Inc.), under the following titles: "Requiem for Holidays," "Chaplin," "Requiem for Radio," "Don't Miss the Next Thrilling Chapter," "Comics," "The Horror of It All," and "Lament for the High Iron."
© Charles Beaumont 1963, 1960, 1960, 1962, 1961, 1959, 1963.

First Printing
Printed in the United States of America

The Macmillan Company, New York
Collier-Macmillan Canada Ltd., Toronto, Ontario

Library of Congress catalog card number: 63-15275

To my friends and fellow mourners
OCee Ritch and Jerry Sohl,
whose contributions to some portions of this book
amounted to collaboration

The author wishes to acknowledge his debt of
gratitude to the following, without whom this
book could not have been written:
OCee Ritch, Jerry Sohl,
Edmond Hamilton, Ray Russell, Frank Robinson,
Hollis Alpert, George Clayton Johnson
and all the many others who have allowed me
to prowl their memory-vaults.

Contents

Holiday song

*Who first invented work, and bound the free
And holiday-rejoicing spirit down . . .*

—CHARLES LAMB

THE RATE of a person's descent into senility can be gauged, it's said, by the degree to which he reminisces. If he harks back to the Good Old Days no more than a couple of dozen times a week, he is considered competent to function; if, however, he is a compulsive reminiscer, forever glorifying the past to the debasement of the present, he is patted on the head and fed soft foods. Certainly he is not taken seriously. Why should he be? Old coots are the same everywhere. Because they've survived the past, they love it, and because they're not at all certain they'll survive the present, they hate it. Of course, that would not be their explanation of the value judgment. To them, the world was indeed a better place when they were young. The girls were prettier then, the men were stronger, the games wilder, the grass greener, the sun

1

warmer, the stairs less steep, and oh! if they could only go back. But they can't, and that's a blessing, because they would find their world as dark and frightening and confusing as the children of today find theirs.

It would be a mistake, however, to ascribe all the maunderings of the compulsive reminiscer to senility. Occasionally his judgments are correct. When the Coot tells you that the girls were prettier, you have only to remember the times you searched through old magazines and photograph albums and decided, at last, that there simply *weren't* any pretty girls before 1940; but when he tells you that they don't build cars in the U.S. Like They Used To, or houses, or toys, you'd better listen. He's right. Those things are gone, probably forever, and their shoddy replacements are all this generation will know. The Stutz Bearcat, the Duesenberg, the rumble-seated Auburn, the Cord sit in cold museums, each a silent reproach to those who dignify today's mobile fashion salons with the word "car." The rock-solid houses, sunk to their knees in the earth, are likewise curiosities, considered impractical by those who make do with the crumbling pink echo-chambers of this age. The lead soldiers have given way to plastic thermonuclear missiles, with convenient destructible cities included at slightly higher cost.

These counterfeits of glories past are saddening. But there is one loss we've sustained which is more than that—it is tragic, for its counterfeit is unquestionably the shoddiest of all.

I speak of the most important, most joyous time of a child's life, any child, anywhere, from the beginning of civilization until recently: the time of the Holiday.

The very word had magic, as it does not any longer. It

had the thunder of fireworks in it, the smell of turkey, the feel of cold sweat forming in the armpits and coursing slowly down the sides; the kaleidoscopic picture of eviscerated pumpkins and horrified neighbors; of running hard in the lowering darkness, away from, toward, it didn't matter; of ghosts and explosions and x's on the calendar ("Only twenty-three more days!") and impossible things like cars on roofs and tin cans sailing clear to the sun and that bike ("For the last time, no! You're too young for a bicycle and, besides, it's much too expensive"). You thought, *Holiday,* and you thought of these things, but mostly you thought of the awful, delicious waiting. Life was little more than that: waiting for the next holiday, feeling the pressure build up inside until it threatened to burst your heart. At night, after the radio programs, after the Big Little books and comics, read by flashlight underneath the covers, you lay awake and planned what to ask for next Christmas, what insidious prank to perpetrate next Halloween, what ruse to employ in order to avoid sharing the Cherry Bombs next Fourth of July. Whoever tasted of that sweet pain will never forget, for no matter how wild the dream, it always came true, which is why the pain was sweet. Holidays were worth it, and more. They were life at its keenest edge, at its heavenly, lawless, joyful best.

Now they are gone. Of course, the world that supported them is gone, too, but who is responsible for that? The kids? Did they ask anyone to take the holidays away? No; they were robbed, and we, the reminiscers, are the culprits, for we are the ones who are making the world of the present. And we ought to be ashamed.

Having created the safe and sane Fourth, the Lifetime

Aluminum Christmas tree, and the trick-or-treat bag, we now sit about drinking Martinis and sighing bitterly about the Kids Nowadays. The fact is, we have a right to sling the booze—but not on their account. The guilt is entirely ours. We are the They who commercialized the holidays, who cheapened them, who tamed them; and we are the They who have got to bring them back.

Enter the Ghosts:

Halloween. Almost nonexistent now, a spiritless, jejune couple of hours one night a year, a shuffling parade of tots in dimestore costumes, each as frightening as Minnie Mouse, a ringing of doorbells, a bit of extortion (carefully observed from the shadows by curiously proud parents), a few nervous giggles; out at seven, in at nine, the end. And what did Halloween used to be? A time to howl, to rage, to scream, to raise the dead and stun the living, long into the dark October night and beyond; a time for rising hackles and gooseflesh; a time for every block in every city and town to become its own Bald Mountain, as the kids were turned loose. God help the parents who asked to come along then: their bones would have been picked clean in a wink. And God help the neighbor who wouldn't let the guys get their football out of his yard, or the storekeeper who wouldn't allow any of his regular customers to swipe a few jawbreakers, or the Truant Officer who just wouldn't. Above all, God help anyone who hadn't the foresight to nail down everything removable. The genies were out of the bottle and the world was theirs.

Genies—or prisoners? For three hundred and sixty-four days of the year we were that, obeying the rules, more or less; but on this day, we rioted. Incredibly, the jailers were good sports about it, too. I doubt that they could have been very happy about the commotion, but they bore up, and sometimes, when they caught you, a strange light would come into their eyes, and they would tell you a few of the things they did when they were kids. And you grew a little, and learned a little, then.

Still, you couldn't believe that past Halloweens were any better. What could be more fantastical than some of the feats of your generation? The ice wagon on the roof of the bandstand cupola—how did it get there? A back-breaking job for a dozen workmen with a crane, impossible for kids. But there it would be the next morning for the rising world to gaze at, all aghast. Perhaps the pyramids were so created, and the other wonders, too.

Of course, we held the strenuous magic to a minimum— show your Power, but don't abuse it; the rest was mischief. Why it didn't land the lot of us in actual jails is difficult to understand. A sample evening: ten masked goblins creeping stealthily up the backstairs of an apartment building, silent as mortal sin, each with a garbage pail; up to the roof, over to the edge; the ten pails suspended for a lovely, giddy moment, then released; another moment of silence, and the sweetest, most marvelous tin thunder ever heard. Lights going on, doors flying open, goblin feet pelting down the stairs, across the littered yard, and on to the next challenge. "Who's got the bag?" "I hid it under my house." An awesome sight: three weeks' accumulation of rotten eggs, dead mice, water balloons, all tucked neatly and invisibly inside an ordinary shopping bag. Out with the bag, over to the Grouch's house. Set the bundle in front of his door, touch a match to it, ring his bell. Hide!

Into the bushes, quick! Here comes Grouch. He sees the burning bag and begins to stamp at it with his feet. Giggles, howls, a terrible oath, and run like hell! "Who's got the lights?" "I got 'em, right here." Over to the building where the Rich People live, the one with the foyer and the speaking tubes and the downstairs door buzzer. Press the little black button; wait. "Yes? Who is it?" Select the biggest lightbulbs in the package. "Who is it, please?" Start dropping the bulbs onto the echoing tile floor. "Don't do it, Rocky, don't kill me!" *Pow!* "I didn't squeal on ya!" *Pow!* "Somebody help me!" *Pow!* "Ya got me!" *Pow, pow pow!* And out, and on.

It was a start, but nothing more: the evening was young. There were privies to be overturned, windows to be soaped and waxed, pins to be stuck in doorbells, horses to be painted, nonexistent ropes to be stretched taut across busy thoroughfares, and, later, young ones to be horrified with the most blood-chilling stories imaginable. The management of the Grand Guignol would have rejected some of those narratives on the grounds that they were too shocking, but the children loved them. They would roam the streets with ticktacks, those notched empty spools with the wind-up string, which made such a lovely racket when run against windows; or with the open-end tin cans and resined cord attachments, excellent for waking the dead; or with scraped-out pumpkins; but, instinctively, they would know when it was story time. They would come running, to an empty field lit by a full moon, or somebody's basement, or an abandoned synagogue, and the serious business of Halloween would begin.

The rule was, it was all right to frighten, to shock and to

surprise, but never to damage. Though some of the boys got carried away and turned hooligan and hoodlum, breaking windows, slashing tires, annoying the sick and the elderly, they were in the minority and their activities were frowned upon by everyone. They broke the Code, which was a rigid one. Most of us knew exactly how far we could and should go. We knew that the lunatic fringe could spoil things for the real pranksters, who had lots of devilment but little malice in their hearts.

It is true that in years past there were jack-o'-lanterns with corn-silk mustaches, and old sheets and hooded masks, but these things were for infants—today's only Halloween participants, if such they can be called. They didn't count. They had nothing to do with the celebration. Then, when a child reached the age of eight, he was turned out to run with the pack this one night of the year, without any admonition to be home early. And he was made to understand by his friends, if he didn't understand already, that vileness was what went on among grownups, not among creatures of his own kind. That is why there was so little damage, and no real vengeance; just a letting off of built-up steam.

And how much steam is let off by shuffling from door to door and mumbling, "Trick or treat," with the treat guaranteed? It is all taken for granted now. Tell the toddlers that you choose to be tricked and they are thrown into confusion, retreating nervously to their fathers or mothers, eight steps away. And thus conformity has dulled the edge of even this tame sport, for the fact is, today's Halloweener doesn't know how to trick. And why should he waste his time thinking about it, anyway, when there are treats, specially prepared for the occasion by the candy manufacturers, waiting at the next house?

A pox on us: we have bribed the children into submissiveness. It is we who have tricked them, and the trick is dirty.

It fills one with uneasiness and apprehension to realize how debased this fine holiday is from what it has been throughout the centuries. The eve of Allhallows, or All Saints' Day, is actually a Christian appropriation of an ancient pagan festival of autumn wherein games, pranks and ghostly tales predominated. It was considered, wisely, to be necessary to the human spirit. The Druids, an order of priests in Gaul and Britain, held their autumn feast at about the same time that the Romans celebrated the festival of Pomona, the goddess of gardens, and other sex-linked events, and the two customs were combined to be perpetuated as Halloween. Perhaps we inherited more from the Romans than from the Druids, for the Romans had an obsession with cruelty that ran through all their festivals, with mischief on the grand scale. The popular and accepted picture of luxurious banquets with harmless indulgences and pleasures is less than accurate. They raised a species of hell beside which our own October evenings were nothing more than lawn parties.

From the Druids we still have the practice of lighting bonfires on the thirty-first, though we've forgotten the attendant superstitions, nor do we follow the habit of feasting on nuts, apples and parsnips. The date was known in Ireland as the Vigil of Saman, and on this night peasants assembled with sticks and clubs and went from house to house collecting money, breadcake, butter, cheese and eggs for the feast. They may not have said, "Trick or treat," but their intentions were clear. In Scotland it was the custom for boys to push the pith from a stalk of cabbage, fill the cavity with tow, set the tow on fire, insert the stalk in the keyhole of the Grouch's house, and blow darts of flame more than a yard in length. If this did not adequately startle him, they would bombard his home with rotten cabbages. The custom of high-jinks on October 31 came to America with every sect and nationality, each with a different heritage, and it was all coalesced into the celebration we knew and loved, the wild, wonderful night of Release, and we have taken this centuries-honored holiday and turned it into a nursery game for diapered tots.

The fate of the Fourth of July is no less sobering.

What started out in 1776 as a unique and stirring day of commemoration, completely American in origin and observance, has declined to just another day off the job, or out of school, a chance to watch a doubleheader in the afternoon and a few pyrotechnic displays in the evening. Absent from the scene are the pulse-quickening brass bands and parades, the flamboyant oratory unflinchingly listened to by great crowds in the heat of the day, with the small boys and their firecrackers on the periphery; the first fried chicken of the year, the best ice cream that ever was (give the freezer one hundred more strokes after the dash gets hard to turn), strawberry pop that cost a nickel for a whole bottle, and the daring mustached balloon ascensionist who climbed into the basket, waved and was whisked off, up and away, by God, while the crowds stood agape.

It was the time of thrills, of distant thunder getting louder, of warm days getting warmer, until the glorious Fourth itself dawned scorching, and the thunder was now, inside you. No ulcers, then, no hypertension. Just the wonderful release of fireworks. With them you would make the loudest bangs ever heard, blast cranky people out of their doldrums, feel the independence that must have stirred the men of the Continental army. And maybe you thought about those men as you lighted your ten-inchers, because the sounds they made were the skirmishing of muskets.

We have different sounds now, and bigger bangs, but they provide no relief of tension. Thinking about them sends a shudder down the spine, for they are sound and fury, signifying nothingness.

Explosions were not presages of imminent obliteration yesterday, so we enjoyed them for their own sake, and ours, and we enjoyed the creation of them. What smell is there now to match the heady, dense aroma of the burning punk you used to light your ladyfingers? What smell to suggest the excitements ahead?

What excitements? the kids today will ask, for they don't know. And how does one express the joy that was felt upon listening to the boom of a flashcracker dropped into a sewer, the echo it made all the way up and down the line, or watching and sniffing that acrid plume of smoke rising gently from the half-moon hole in the manhole cover?

How do you describe the look on the face of the streetcar motorman when he ran over the torpedoes you set in his tracks? Surprised, you say; annoyed, but patient, tolerant, full of memories of his own, how it used to be with him this day . . . but it's no good. The look has disappeared.

Oh, the Fourth of July was a fine day, you want to tell this generation, a fine, wonderful, violent day. There was the smell of burnt gunpowder in the air, always, and the only silence the short wait between explosions, all over the country.

"What did you do?" the kids ask.

Well, you lighted firecrackers underneath cans and you ran a few steps and turned and watched the cans fly up.

You buried firecrackers up to their fuses in dirt and set them off.

"Didn't you get dirty?"

Very.

"What else?"

Well, you played with sons-o'-guns.

"What are——"

Little red wafers about the size of a penny. You stepped on them with your heel and then whirled yourself around and around while they snapped and hissed and banged in a fury, and the girls all held their ears.

"Go on."

You held ladyfingers in your hand and, with great daring and arrogance, touched the punk to them; and they would begin to sizzle, but you wouldn't let go——

"Didn't they go off in your hand?"

Yes, but they didn't hurt, if you knew how to hold them: loosely, at the very ends.

You shot off rockets, of course. And hurled Cherry Bombs.

"We've still got those!"

No, you don't. Our Cherry Bombs were glittery red grenades that exploded on contact with any unyielding surface, such as, say, a passing coal truck. But it was the firecrackers that we loved best. They came in all different sizes, one-inchers

to ten-inchers, and you bought them in packets at any dime-
store. First you ripped off the paper, which was an odd, crinkly
wax-colored paper that came from Japan, usually, with funny
drawings of American children with Oriental eyes, and then
you started taking the 'crackers apart. They had their long
white fuses knotted together, and——

"Weren't they dangerous?"

Sure, but that was part of the fun.

"They're against the law."

The history books say we won the American Revolution,
but it appears that big segments of the independence we fought
for are being lost.We let them talk us out of sharing the risks
of the Continental troops, and a bit of that glory, when we
let them (us) outlaw firecrackers. True, there were accidents,
injuries, even deaths, but they did not come close to the number we see today—mostly incurred in automobiles going to
and from the beaches, the picnic grounds and those parks where
they have the fireworks displays. In the outlaw years, every
kid with the meagerest smattering of intelligence knew enough
to leave a dud alone. Who didn't know enough to get out of
the way of the cascading brilliance of Roman candles? Everybody did.

The dangers were not so much with the regular fireworks
as with the homemade variety. For a few cents you could get
horse capsules and a generous supply of potassium chlorate
and red phosphorous from the corner drugstore, and the
pharmacist wouldn't bat an eye when you asked for it. You
went home with your purchase, then, and packed your own
torpedoes by mixing the ingredients and inserting them in the
capsules. Wherever thrown, they would go off with a resound-

ing blast—almost as good as Cherry Bombs. The only thing was, you had to be careful not to make any jerky movements or they would go off in your pockets, which sometimes happened. Then there was potassium chlorate and sulphur. In the right combination, this mixture could be detonated with a brick, a stone, or a hammer, and the resulting bang was often better than anything provided by the manufacturers. Here again, technique was involved. Certain incautious children were occasionally rendered *hors de combat* by backflying bricks, stones and hammers.

There were few homemade rockets, but there were plenty of innovations in the matter of sending them off. Rainspouts were preferred, and a six-foot drainpipe was a thing to treasure all year as the ideal Fourth of July launching pad. You could buy two rockets for as little as four pennies or as much as three dollars. The expensive ones had shellbursts. It made you feel uneasy to see your money going up in smoke, but when you saw the magnificent star-filled trail across the night sky, and the explosion of color at the apogee, you knew it was worth it.

That was a time when nobody thought boys were by nature obedient, cheerful, or kind. Boys were considered, with perfect reason, scamps, rascals, young devils. Their boundless energy was the dismay of their elders, who knew that it had to be spent somehow, else it would implode. So everyone thought it completely natural that the kids should release their tensions with firecrackers, pinwheels, and the whole catalogue of noisemakers; not only natural but salubrious. Dad, who was always close with his money, could be counted on to lay in a big supply. You knew what you wanted, you told him what to get, but he invariably overextended himself when you got him to the fireworks stand. The only real problem then was to keep him from shooting them all off himself.

You had the long, full day of explosions, and then you crawled into bed at night, dirty, exhausted, sometimes bandaged and blistered; and you arose the next morning miraculously free of frustrations, satisfied with yourself, ready, if not precisely willing, to cope with the gray unrealities. The battle had been won, but the war was still in progress—you against peace and quiet—and there would always be this holiday.

What remains of the Grand and Glorious Fourth? Certainly none of the color, or very little of it: here and there an American flag, the occasional faraway thump of a smuggled 'cracker, but mostly quiet streets, deserted cities, a few family picnics, perhaps a band concert or two, and a total absence of pageantry. The kids spend the day now at the beaches, or the community swimming pools, or in front of their television sets, where they are every other day of summer. The only difference is the lethargic half-hour or so they devote to the legal fireworks—a pale, hissing ghost of the assortments of yesterday—and the evening trip to the park. There, if you have the stomach to fight the crowds, the strangers and the nostalgia, you can see—at a discreet distance—displays that might have been staged by Ziegfeld. They are as lovely as flower gardens, and approximately as exciting. That this is true is borne out by the fact that they get shorter and shorter every year, and less imaginative. There is the five-hundred-dollar display, the thousand-dollar display, and maybe, if the town is large enough, the two-thousand-dollar display, which generally lasts thirty minutes. The money for these nods toward the past is extracted from merchants and city treasurers, most of whom bewail the pointless expense. Judging from their public comments, one would assume that they regard the custom of shooting off fireworks on the Fourth as a ridiculous waste of time and cash.

President John Adams once said, "I am apt to believe that it [Independence Day] will be celebrated by succeeding generations as the great anniversary festival. It ought to be commemorated as the day of deliverance, by solemn acts of devotion to God Almighty. It ought to be solemnized with pomp and parade, with shows, games, sports, guns, bells, bonfires, and illuminations, from one end of this continent to the other, from this time forward for evermore." That it is not so celebrated is no fault of that misunderstood patriot. The early Independence Days *were* occasions for shows, games, sports; for military music and fireworks; but in 1954 Congress passed an act prohibiting the transportation of fireworks into any state where their sale is forbidden, which was soon almost all the states, and that was the end of the holiday. Once again, Americans withdrew from the role of participants and became, as in so many other areas, spectators. But, as we see, soon there may be nothing for them to look at.

Even so innocent a holiday as St. Valentine's Day has been subrogated by do-gooders who don't want to see anybody hurt, and by commercial interests. The day persists despite the fact that it is no holiday at all, nobody gets out of school, nobody gets a day off work because of it. Yet stores devote more space to Valentine's Day than they do to most of the other holidays.

It never was much talked about. Boys pretended it didn't exist, except perhaps as a scheme, on the part of silly and detested girls, to embarrass them. They winced and grimaced at the very mention of the occasion. Yet Valentine's Day accounted for the first stirrings of exultant joy and suicidal pain which could not be linked to any past experience. Of course no boy would ever admit to anything but contempt for the practice of handing out the little heart-shaped cards, but each secretly hoped that he would get one. If he did, he would strike a sneering posture (after making sure that his friends were apprised of his fortune) and, more often than not, tear the idiot thing into a dozen pieces. If he did not, he would lie and say that he had. And that night he would go to bed blinking away the tears, more certain than ever of his outcast state.

The stirrings were sexual, and in a peculiar, instinctive way, the boys knew it, even though they didn't know what sexual was. It was the Time of Humiliation, when your body began to betray you, but you couldn't see the connection. Every boy in puberty has known the unspeakable horror of having his imminent manhood stiffen and rise, like a disembodied thing over which he has no control, on the school bus, or a minute before the English teacher calls him up to the blackboard to diagram a sentence, or at church. And every boy has spoken silently to the abominable member, pleading with it, commanding it, entreating it, to no avail. Nothing ever worked. Neither thinking about "other things," as someone had advised, nor exerting physical pressure. It always remained at attention just long enough to flood the boy's face with red as, with one hand plunged into his pocket, he attempted to look casual.

Valentine's Day was the time for that trauma as no other

time was. The boys avoided each other's eyes and blushed and the girls giggled.

It was awful, and, once you found out that you were not the only one so afflicted, it was wonderful.

It may be that Valentine's Day was begun in honor of this awakening. While its origin has been lost in antiquity, it has been traced to the Roman Lupercalia, which were feasts held in February, to honor Pan and Juno. At that time it was the custom to place the names of young women in a box and to have these names drawn out by young men as chance directed. The girls became the men's "valentines" for an entire year, during which time gifts and favors were exchanged, with no limits imposed or expected. The Christian clergy, finding the practice less than pleasing, introduced a modification: they substituted the names of saints for those of girls. But they did not reckon with the nature of pubescent and post-pubescent males. Within a very short time, the saints were returned to their perpetual abode and the girls brought out again. It was an altogether satisfactory arrangement, achieving the status of *the* holiday in France and England during the sixteenth century.

Actually, there were two St. Valentines, and neither was a specialist in affairs of the heart. The first was a Roman priest who stood steadfast to his faith during the Claudian persecutions and was, in consequence, beaten with clubs and then beheaded. What is left of him is preserved in the church of St. Praxedes in Rome. The second St. Valentine was a Roman bishop and he fared no better, suffering decapitation a few years after the first. Either gentleman would no doubt be surprised to find himself a lover's saint.

In the seventeenth century it became the custom for a man to give a woman a present if he was challenged by her with the words, "Good morrow, 'tis St. Valentine's Day." From Samuel Pepys we get the first record of what would become the modern valentine, also an insight into a charming, vanished custom. He writes (February 14, 1667): "This morning came up to my wife's bedside little Will Mercer to be her valentine, and brought her name writ upon blue paper, in gold letters, done by himself and very pretty; and we were both well pleased with it."

What has happened in the interval was, of course, inevitable. Valentine's Day has become a negligible and vanishing custom, reserved for that species known as the Pre-Teen. It slouches into the drugstore, grabs up a haphazard collection of cheap cards—some egregiously sentimental, some sadistic (known as "Un-Valentine cards"), all abominably rhymed ("This is the time / For you to know / I love you so / My Valentine")—and slouches over to the post office. A few signatures, into the slot with the bundle, and out; the end.

Old Cootism? Senility? Perhaps, but only if the sexual awakening has been moved back to the ages of eight, nine and ten, which is possible but, I should think, doubtful. At any rate, that is the age group to which Valentine's Day is presently confined, and before long I expect the five-year-olds to claim it as their personal property. Which suggests to me that it has lost a bit of its original meaning.

Christmas has lost *all* of its original meaning, fortunately. As we shall see, the celebration began as a sort of bacchanal, bearing even less resemblance to the holiday we remember than the present debacle, though of the two, I'm not so sure I don't prefer the former. It had, at least, the virtue of spontaneity. It had joy and excitement. And the lack of these qualities is what has ruined, or is ruining, Christmas.

Expurgated reference works tell us that December 25 was already a festive day for the sun god Mithra and appealed to Christians as an appropriate date to commemorate the birth of Jesus, "The Light of the World," around A.D. 534. Some theologians, of course, deny this, claiming the day to be nothing more nor less than the date of Christ's birth. However, other historical scholars hold that the time of the winter solstice throughout recorded history was something else entirely. The Romans' Saturnalia began on December 17 and continued for a week with no limits imposed, the point being total abandonment of inhibitions. Then there is the Feast of Fools, which was celebrated on Christmas Day until the time of Queen Elizabeth. This occasion was replete with the slinging of excrement, displays of transvestitism, and a general sexual license, with all social classes joining in. Shocking to the civilized modern, it was considered by its participants nothing more than another holiday, very orgiastic hence very cathartic, and not taken in the least seriously. Perhaps the favorite sport, equivalent, say, to trimming the tree, was stripping down naked and going about the streets in a manure cart, pelting people with dung. Presumably it was done in the same high spirit of good fun as the snowballing of our own time. Everybody ducked, as they do today, and no one was offended, either at what was hurled or by the lewd postures effected by the cart riders. History is filled with similar festivals on this most cherished holiday, and all partook similarly of the salutary effects of expressed hysteria, harmless violence and sexual activity.

Let it not be thought that I am espousing a cause, as Freud once remarked at the conclusion of a lively chapter on perversions. I do not hanker for a return to those celebrations but, rather, to an approximation of the joyful spirit out of which they sprang.

We have a touch of it in the traditional, and much despised, Christmas office party, but it is only a touch, and it is weakening every year. An example of this decline may be seen in the Hollywood motion-picture studios. Ten years ago they all used to abandon their We're-just-ordinary-folks pose and stage the wildest, most orgiastic day-before-Christmas parties one could hope for. At Universal-International, the Writers' Building, an otherwise grim edifice, somewhat reminiscent of San Quentin, became a Palace of Joy, or sin, depending upon your view of these things. Weary, bitter, frightened scenarists could be observed hooting down the halls after the same secretaries they'd worked with, and never noticed, for three hundred and sixty-four days. Flint-hearted producers offered seven-year contracts to girls who dreamed, but never really believed, that they would rise above their status as messengers. Actors told their directors what they really thought of them, and vice versa, whereupon they would exchange blows and then, usually, fall weeping into each other's arms, the best of friends. It was Midnight, and the masks came off, for a little while. A few days later, of course, they were back on again; but there was a difference.

Now the masks stay on. At M-G-M last year, veteran studio employees were dismayed, as they had every right to be, by the following notice:

To All Departments:
Any employee who is discovered to be in the possession of any alcoholic beverage whatsoever shall be subject to dismissal. This is a
working day.

The day referred to was the day before Christmas.

And what is the foundation of our Christmas hebephrenia,
our fear of parties, our inability to express those areas of ourselves that, psychologists insist, demand expression? Is it that
we have mistaken the point of civilization and assumed it to
mean the suppression of all natural tendencies?

I think so. I think that in this sophisticated age we have
come to equate pleasure with sin and displeasure with virtue.
It may be the heritage left us by the Puritan founders. To them,
as we know, morality was a simple matter: the more difficult
the task, the greater the benefit. Yet these good, gray Puritans
did not originate the concept of the desirability of repressed
emotions. It has been with us, to one degree or another, from
the beginning; if it hadn't, there would have been no Saturn-
alias, no orgies, no holidays, in the first place. They were insti-
tuted as corrective measures, meant to take care of the necessary
imbalance we had imposed upon Nature. If anyone is to blame,
it's the Serpent.

But I think we are taking the curse too far, making more of
it than we have to. If we cannot follow Childe Rolande's advice
and "let joy be unconfined," at least we can let it out into the
sunlight a few times a year. By all means let us make use of our
inhibitions most of the time; it is through them that we have
achieved the better part of our glory; but let us, for God's sake,
understand that the greatest glory, as well as the lowest bestial-
ity, comes of breaking through these inhibitions. The whole of

art, at its highest, has been created by men who have chafed at their restrictions, burst free of them, and felt fulfilled—or, as it so often happened, burdened with guilt.

Guilt is the key, but we are applying it to the wrong door. Instead of feeling shame for what we did in our lost holidays, we should feel shame for not allowing the new generation the same privilege. They will die with regrets anyway, as people have done from the beginning of time, but the regrets will be over the things they have not done, and that is the worst feeling of all.

It is probably too late to prevent it from happening, but we could try.

We could turn the kids loose on Halloween and tell them not to show their faces in the house till after midnight; we could bring back firecrackers and brass bands; we could keep the girl-children out of brassières until they're ready for them, and let the boys discover sex in their own time; and we could revive the institution of the unrestrained Christmas party.

Maybe the result would be that the kids, and we, ourselves, would simply be embarrassed; that we would realize we were trying to bring back, not a past era, nor some grand traditions, but our youth.

And maybe not.

A first, relatively easy step would be to halt the decline of Christmas in its classic form. Shake it loose from its current position as a status game and give it back to the kids. Forbid any Santa Claus to appear publicly before December 15, remembering that children can accommodate belief in the department store variety along with belief in the real Saint Nick, if they're given half a chance. Ban all parades until a week before The

The little fellow

HIGH ON the list of America's pet hates is a man who, over a thirty-year period, gave this nation— and every other nation in the world—a gift valuable beyond price and beyond estimation, the most desirable and most difficult to receive: the imperishable gift of joy.

There was a time when Charlie Chaplin's name was a synonym for happiness. Now, and inevitably, it is a symbol of hatred and a monument—as if we needed one—to humanity's eternal and passionate ingratitude. Chaplin spent the fruitful years of his life preaching a sermon to the heart. Good and evil were not part of the sermon, its point being that good and evil do not exist, that only joy exists. Now, in transcendent irony, we are told that Chaplin is an evil man. It is being said, by aging female journalists, by pettifogging senators, by hacks, and other self-appointed spokesmen of the American people, that he is a bad sort—or, as the one-time Attorney General of the United States, James P. McGranery, put it, "an

unsavory character." In 1952 Chaplin embarked upon a vacation cruise with his wife. Two days later, instructions were
issued to the Immigration authorities to hold the actor for a
hearing to determine whether or not he would be allowed to
re-enter the country. Chaplin, said McGranery, speaking for
the nation, "has been publicly charged with being a member
of the Communist Party, with grave moral charges and with
making statements that would indicate a leering, sneering
attitude toward a country whose hospitality has enriched
him."

There were a few dissenting voices, a few citizens who felt
that it was America that had been enriched, but the majority
appeared to be delighted at Chaplin's exile. The columnists, as
though to stem the tide of sympathy, pointed out that the
Attorney General had been kind in his judgments. They reminded us, in great but vague detail, of Chaplin's sins. He was
a Commie. He was a tax dodger. He was a ravisher of young
girls. He was an atheist. Worst of all, he was ungrateful. After
forty years in this country, had he had the common decency
to take out American citizenship papers? No! Clearly, it was
a case of good riddance to bad rubbish.

Since 1952, Chaplin has lived abroad. With only the slightest
trace of rancor, he has stated that he does not intend to return
to the United States. While his attitude toward us might be one
of profound bitterness, of outrage and disgust, he has said nothing to indicate that this is so. Instead, with the exception of a
controversial film called *A King in New York,* he has maintained a dignified silence. In a gesture reminiscent of another,
greater Charlie—the little fellow Chaplin created and who
danced his way into the affections of all who saw him—Chaplin

simply shrugged off the tragedy, turned his back, and disappeared.

But for this, the press might have reversed its approach. Like other nations, we are given to great kindness once we have administered punishment and exacted contrition. But to forgive forgiveness! The Big Mama columnists asked only for an expression of sorrow and a perhaps halfhearted promise of better behavior. Receiving the shrug instead, they tucked in their ample bosoms and bared their fangs. An anti-Chaplin campaign was begun, calculated by its emphases and omissions to present a single image of Chaplin, so hateful an image that some European critics concluded that it was a classic admission of guilty conscience.

Of course, people believed what they read. Even so, it was possible to think of *Chaplin* as a wretched little alien and still enjoy *Charlie* on the screen. For a while. Then the campaign began to have its success. Not content to destroy the man, the columnists proceeded to attack the man's work. Learned students of the cinema, such as Hedda Hopper, began to have second thoughts about the "so-called Chaplin masterpieces." Were they really so great? Were they really as funny as they were cracked up to be?

Despite the encouraging success of the recently reissued *Modern Times* and *The Gold Rush*, a number of small but alarming fissures have begun to appear in the estimation of Chaplin's professional achievements. Only a few months ago, a logorrheac Hollywood TV personality was asked why he persisted in slamming Chaplin. "I'll tell you," said the personality. "I've got nothing against the guy personally. What he does is his own business. I'm just sick of hearing all this stuff about what a great comic he was. You seen one of his pictures recently? They're pathetic. Stupid. What's funny about a little schmo who looks like Hitler and acts like a queer? I'll tell you a great comic. Joey Frisco. There's a great comic. . . ."

So now even Charlie—as distinct from Chaplin—is under attack. It would be comforting to think the Little Fellow isn't in danger, that nothing so magnificent could possibly perish, but other magnificent things have perished, and at the hands of men. Why not Charlie too? Film doesn't last forever, and memory fades. And though we speak of a wonder that held the world enchanted for three generations, the wonder has demonstrably begun to dim. The young in America today do not know Chaplin at all, except as the monster the press has built, and that is sad. Unless they live in the few great cities of the nation, they do not know Charlie, either. And that is tragic. For the artist and his art, separable as they may and must be, are of vital importance to the cultural and moral development of America. If we allow ourselves to forget what we had, then we shall never understand what we lost, and that will make us poor indeed.

"I have a notion that he suffers from a nostalgia of the slums." So wrote Somerset Maugham of his friend Charles Spencer Chaplin, touching upon one of the great secrets of Chaplin's art. From the beginning it has been a celebration and a mockery of the earth's poor. Celebration because while we breathe, even in the dankest air of the lowest slum, we live, and life is sacred; mockery because, in Chaplin's words, "The poor deserve to be mocked! What fools they are!" What holy fools, he should have added, for that must be the final description of his masterpiece, Charlie.

But Maugham was also stating a literal truth. Chaplin's formative years were spent in the East End of London, where he was taken when barely a year old from his birthplace, Fontainebleau. Kennington was then, and is now, a gray, dismal, squalid crowd of ancient buildings, infested by the poor, the sick, the lame and the ignorant. Chaplin's father was a music-hall entertainer of slender talents. His income was small and most of it went for liquor. He died before the new century, and Chaplin remembers standing all night long outside St. Thomas' hospital, where his father lay, waiting for the light from the unshuttered window to go out. When it finally did go out, Chaplin's mother, Hannah, was faced with the nearly impossible task of supporting herself and her two sons.

The elder son, Sydney, Charles' half-brother (and for whom Charles' best-known son is named), achieved a certain fame of his own and accompanied Charles to America, eventually becoming his general manager and business manager. In the course of an interview, Sydney once made a number of disparaging remarks about their early life, putting some of the blame upon his mother. Charles, who was present, went into a cold rage and banished Sydney from the room. Later, he explained: "They can say what they want about my mother—she was greater than I will ever be. She *was* a great actress. I've never seen anyone like her—she was good to me when I was a kid—she gave me all she had—and asked nothing back —and by Heaven, I've got no mother complex either. She was just a good fellow."

Under the stage name of Lily Harley, Hannah Chaplin performed in Gilbert and Sullivan stock companies, but her earnings were low and the strain finally broke her. She tried sewing, but even this light work fatigued her. When Charles was six years old, Hannah suffered a series of mental collapses. She was taken to an institution, and her sons were left to fend for themselves. Alone in the city, Charles plunged directly to the hard core of survival, wandering the cold streets in search of scraps, struggling constantly to stay alive so that he might enjoy the occasional visits he was permitted with his mother. From time to time she would be released and they would live together in a workhouse, but these relatively happy periods never lasted long. For nine more years Hannah alternated between the workhouse and the hospital, her condition growing steadily worse. Yet, as Chaplin recalls, "she never lost her sense of humor." And he thanks this quality of his mother's for his own extraordinary ability to stay afloat during those hard times.

"She had the most marvelous gift of mimicry; I learned everything from her. We would sit in our drab little room and the people would pass below and mother would mimic them, giving an elaborate history of each as he or she would pass. . . ."

With such an inheritance, it is perhaps natural that Chaplin became interested in the theatre almost as soon as he could talk. At the age of seven, he haunted the London stages, watching the crowds, worshiping the performers with whom he felt a deep kinship. He claims now that his talent for pantomime was fully developed before he was ten, and that he never for a moment doubted that he would devote his life to entertainment. He entertained people from the time of his earliest memory and somehow he knew that he had a very special talent—although of course he didn't know precisely what it was.

Getting a job in the theatre was even more difficult then than it is now. After short stints as newsboy, toymaker and

lather boy in a barber shop, Charles went looking for engage-
ments. Hannah thought he was too young for the hard professional life, but at last she relented and, through her remaining contacts, arranged for him to join the Eight Lancashire
Lads, a troupe of child clog dancers. By the time he was eight,
Charles was a veteran showman. He stayed with the troupe for
two more years, and, after playing in a large number of variety
shows, landed a small part in William Gillette's famous drama-
tization of *Sherlock Holmes*. He toured with the company for
four years, then appeared, as one of the wolves, in the first
performance of Barrie's *Peter Pan*. Meanwhile, Sydney was
doing well, also in the theatre. Which is to say, both were
making enough—barely enough—to survive without having to
resort to theft or charity.

In 1906, when he was seventeen, Charles was appearing in
most of the music halls as a regular performer. He had a solo
act, with songs, and was considered one of England's outstanding young talents—but hardly in the same league with his
brother. Sydney was tiring of the fight and so was delighted to
accept an offer from Fred Karno, king of the music halls. At
a grand three pounds per week, Sydney felt that he had
achieved the nearest thing to security in the entertainment business. He was happy with the Karno company and, once solidly
entrenched, asked the impresario to hire Charles.

Karno had doubts. The younger Chaplin did not appear, at
first glance, to have much potential as a comic. But when he
went through one of his routines, shedding the sickly, serious
seventeen-year-old exterior like a snake's winter skin, and exploding into a combination tumbler, acrobat, singer, dancer,
mimic and jokester, Karno hired him at once, without misgiv-

ing. This was to prove the first important development in Chaplin's professional career.

He was an instantaneous success in the troupe, largely because of the freedom Karno allowed him in the sketches. Most of these would seem unbearably quaint today, but Chaplin admits that they helped form much of his future style. It was with Karno that he learned the immense theatrical value of seemingly insignificant detail. Picking a daisy is a commonplace and unremarkable action, by itself; inserted into the right context it can become an action of the most overpowering significance. (In a *City Lights* sequence, Charlie, stoned to the keel, is being dragged home by a friend who is only one degree less pixilated; en route, Charlie notices a daisy, picks it and holds it to his nose; the screen fairly bursts with joy.) He learned timing, also, and all the magic graces which he later brought to perfection.

After a few years, Karno sent Charles to America for an extended tour, and the second and most decisive development of his career occurred. America had fallen in love with the movies. There were film dramas, but the cry was for film comedy, and the producers could not turn out enough humorous pictures to meet the demand. A horse-faced, impish talent named Mack Sennett was the unchallenged emperor of this new field. He produced one- and two-reel comedies at the rate of three per week, but somehow he managed to instill in each zaniness and quality. His stable of comics—Ford Sterling, Roscoe "Fatty" Arbuckle, Buster Keaton, Chester Conklin, Mabel Normand, et al., together with the immortal Keystone Cops—had become an American habit, and would-be competitors found the door solidly shut against them.

No one knows what Sennett's secret was, including Sennett. His only philosophy toward comedy was that it ought to be fun to watch. In line with this approach, it struck him that watching the same actors over and over again was not much fun, so he conducted an unending search for fresh talent—in all departments. He saw Chaplin's act at the Pantages Theatre in Los Angeles, thought it was pretty good, but not good enough to do anything about. Several months later, Mack's Number One comic, Ford Sterling, began to complain. Not realizing that it was the Sennett touch and not the work of any single performer that made the films successful, Sterling demanded a huge raise. Sennett demurred, on the grounds that, if he gave it to Sterling, then everybody else would expect the same thing. Sterling grumbled some threats, and Sennett started to look for a replacement. Scraping his brain for ideas, he suddenly remembered the little cockney he'd seen with the Karno group at the Pantages. Recalling nothing except a certain enthusiasm he'd felt at the time, he told his publicity men to find "a guy called Chapman or Chipton or something like that" and promptly forgot about it. In a few weeks, he was told that Charles Chaplin was working for a pittance in Oil City, Pennsylvania.

Without bothering to take another look, Sennett instructed his men to offer Chaplin a year's contract at $75 per week. Chaplin was then making $50, and the increase looked appealing. However, he was basically an entertainer, and although he had been amused and interested by the early film experiments of Max Linder, he couldn't bring himself to regard the flickering business seriously. Besides, with Karno he had security.

Having given the matter a little thought, Chaplin refused

Sennett's offer—by way of demanding triple the amount. To his surprise, the demand was met, and in this manner Charles Chaplin backed into the medium he was to lift to the highest degree of art.

It wasn't art then. The Keystone comedians were all masters of slapstick, but that was about the extent of their talent. They leaped and ran and rolled about the screen like wild wind-up toys, falling down, getting up, falling down again, and relying always upon utter chaos for their effect. Sometimes it worked, sometimes—no one can say why—it didn't.

The trouble was, none of it was even remotely Chaplin's style. When the British comedian strode shyly into the studio to report for work, Sennett, like Karno before him, was positive he'd made a mistake. How would this pale, sensitive young man ever fit in with the wild loonies and their pies-in-the-face? Daunted, the great producer sighed, dispatched his latest acquisition and made a successful effort to put the blunder out of his mind.

This reaction was a fortunate thing, for us all. Had Sennett been impressed, he would have prepared a series of his own devising for Chaplin, and Charlie might never have been. As it was, the new actor was free to experiment. His first picture, *Making a Living,* was in every way a disaster. Typically Keystone Coppian, it ran its chaotic mile with Chaplin appearing as a dude in a Chinese mustache; there was nothing funny nor individual from first to last foot of film, and no hint whatever of the Little Fellow.

Sennett was not surprised, but Chaplin admits that the experience was personally crushing to him. He had managed to convince himself that motion pictures could provide a fine showcase for his talents, but now it appeared that he would vanish into the great panicking crowd of funnymen. He brooded about the matter at length, taking many midnight walks through the poorer sections of Los Angeles. Gradually, faintly, an idea formed. He knew that it would sound bad, even if he were able to verbalize it, so he decided to develop it thoroughly on his own and then give it, whole, to Sennett.

The idea took shape the following week. From the London beggars who had haunted his youth, he would make a composite figure. In this figure would be all the elements which had frightened and amused him: the ragtag clothes, the dirt, the air of absolute and irrevocable failure, the pathetic dignity. He took Mack Swain's walrus mustache first and began cutting it down. By accident—the only accident in Charlie's creation— he went too far and ended with nothing more than a square patch. But it looked right. To this he added Fatty Arbuckle's bowler hat and gigantic trousers, and Ford Sterling's oversized shoes. The bamboo cane was an afterthought. Together, amazingly, the stray odds and ends made a perfectly homogeneous ensemble. It took only a bit of white make-up (descended from death-conscious clowns in the times of the great plagues) to convince Chaplin that he had found the perfect answer.

Charlie was born.

He came of cast-off clothes and desperation, but he was an embodiment: his spirit may be traced back to all the other great embodiments of joy: through Joseph Grimaldi, Dan Leno, Jean-Gaspard Duburau, whose sweet foolery similarly charmed and convulsed audiences; back further through Don Quixote, Punch, Pierrot, and finally, Pan himself. Pan danced through life, reminding man of the joy of his mortality. So did Charlie.

So do all the really great clowns. Life is strong in them and they celebrate it.

Only a creation of the highest art can express joy in the *whole* of life, which is not cruel and is not mean and is not kind, but is all these things. Charlie the tramp eloquently expressed this. It is what separated him—and separates him—from such other grand and wonderful clowns as Buster Keaton, Harry Langdon, Harold Lloyd, W. C. Fields, Laurel and Hardy, Raimu, and Cantinflas.

He does not cut a dashing figure as he blunders through a drab and commonplace existence [wrote Chaplin of Charlie]. Heroism with him, except on great occasions, never soars to greater heights than his interviews with his landlord. His fortunes always drag a little behind his expectations, and fulfillment lies always out of reach. And as he shambles along with dwindling hopes he is smitten more than ever with a sense of his own unfitness and inadequacy. When [the common man] sees on the stage or screen the romantic hero who sweeps through life like a whirlwind, he feels a sense of inferiority and is depressed. Then he sees me shuffling along in my baffled and aimless manner, and a spark of hope rekindles. Here is a man like himself, only more pathetic and miserable, with ludicrously impossible clothes—in every sense a misfit and a failure. The figure on the screen has a protective air of mock dignity—takes the most outrageous liberties with people—and wears adversity as though it were a bouquet. . . .

He wears adversity as though it were a bouquet. . . . Charlie's world was full of adversities, and tragedies, yet he survived them, triumphantly, and this is why everyone loved him. They warmed to the truth of Charlie's Law: the survival of the unfittest.

It is unfair to blame Mack Sennett for not immediately recognizing the magnificence of this. After all, the success of Keystone was rooted firmly in slapstick, and it is not always wise to tamper with success. Nonetheless, his fears notwithstanding, Sennett approved the costume and allowed Chaplin to wear it in his next picture, *The Kid Auto Races at Venice*.

Amid all the flailing arms and rolling eyes, the little tramp figure appeared as a divine thunderbolt. With a wink he toppled Sterling from his throne as America's favorite clown and demolished the rest of the competition. Of course, Charlie was not fully realized in this early effort (released February 7, 1914), but Chaplin knew that it was only a matter of time. He was aware that there was significance in the character he had invented and that it might take him a lifetime to understand this significance.

His next thirty-five pictures for Keystone were instantaneous hits. Chaplin's name became famous before the year was through, and when it was time for contract renewal he requested a raise, on brother Syd's advice. Sennett refused, for the same reasons that had prompted him to refuse Sterling: it would set a dangerous precedent. Years later, Sennett admitted his mistake, but claimed that he had been right at the time. Of Chaplin he said, simply, "Oh, he's just the greatest artist that ever lived, that's all."

Within a few months, Chaplin was working for the Essanay company in Chicago, at $1,250 per week. Shortly thereafter, he signed a contract with Mutual for the unheard-of salary of $10,000 per week, plus bonuses. All this while he concentrated upon developing the character of the Little Fellow, adding the refinements that were to make Charlie the most magnificent comic character of the century. Chaplin understood that true art cannot be collaborative, and so he insisted upon writing (*making up,* more properly; there were no scripts in those days) and directing his films.

Such masterpieces as *The Bank* and *The Floorwalker* caused Chaplin's fame to spread, and before World War I had begun, he was acknowledged to be the most popular man in the world. In a recent attack, *The Saturday Evening Post* quotes Chaplin as having commented: "I am known in lamaseries where the name Jesus Christ has never been heard." The *Post* regards this as an incredible and somewhat sacrilegious boast. It is nothing of the kind. Thanks to the invention of motion pictures and to the universal language he spoke, Charles Chaplin might well lay claim to being the first man truly world famous in his time. Not even the greatest figures before him could be certain of immediate recognition in every civilized community on earth.

During the war, Chaplin put Charlie to work selling Liberty Bonds, and raised more money for this country than any other individual. He also raised a great deal of money for himself, and very soon was able to assume complete control of his career. With the forming of United Artists, which was his idea, and the construction of a private studio at La Brea and Sunset in Hollywood, he became the first independent star-producer.

His films continued to enjoy success. So high was the level of their artistry that they left no area of the audience uncaptured. The intellectuals began to see in Chaplin a new messiah, and the people—all the people, all over the world—accepted him as they accepted the sun. Masterpiece followed masterpiece. And though the level of quality was not invariable, it can be said that each film contained more invention, more originality, and more downright fun than a year's production of other companies.

With the exception of *Woman of Paris,* a Chaplin-directed film in which neither Charlie nor Chaplin appeared, these pictures comprised a chronicle of the Little Fellow's adventures, and became part of the world's culture.

Chaplin was now rich and powerful. Though but a short time out of the Kennington slums, he found himself an object of veneration. Dispensing love, he received love in return; and his fame grew, like a vast silvery balloon.

That this must have its effect upon a man is, or should be, self-evident. Chaplin the man had always been withdrawn. The sudden overwhelming popularity caused him to withdraw further. People did not understand. They did not understand that Chaplin's way of repaying them for their love was to give them the best of him, through Charlie, and that having put into Charlie all that was wild and fine and sweet in him, there was little left over.

But people have a way of resenting great artists. A man may travel to the searing center of his soul and come out with a new vision, and the world will ask him why he hasn't changed his shirt.

This is what the world—our American world—began to ask Chaplin. Over a twenty-year period, working twenty hours a day, he was making the finest films anyone had ever seen, distilling his genius to its greatest perfection in such unforgettable scenes as the dance of the rolls and the eating of the shoe in *The Gold Rush,* the blind girl's first glimpse of the tramp in *City Lights,* the automatic feeder in *Modern Times,* the globe-map ballet in *The Great Dictator.* And the people laughed, but they did not forgive. For while Chaplin was dishing up these delights, he was living a life described by columnists as "unnormal."

To ask an artist to please everyone with his life as well as his art is both stupid and unfair. Even if all the charges leveled against Chaplin were true, America's attitude would be difficult to understand. As the charges are almost entirely false, the attitude is inexplicable.

What, in fact, were his sins?

They say he is—or was—a Communist. That is not so. It has never been so. Along with most of the intelligent people of his time, Chaplin was grieved at the inequality of the world and took an interest in all theories which proposed to end that inequality; but he never joined nor promoted in any way the Communist party. While it is certainly true that, from one viewpoint, his films were a protest against the uneven distribution of wealth, it is also true that many intellectuals were protesting against the same shameful condition. Politically, Chaplin's pictures, which stress *personal* freedom, displeased the Soviet government far more than the American. Careful research reveals that his closest tie with Marxism was his friendship with the great Russian film director, Sergei Eisenstein, who said Chaplin was "able to see . . . the most tragic things through the eyes of a laughing child." Together they plotted nothing more sinister than a possible film collaboration, which never came off.

To the charge of ingratitude, it is difficult to reply. In 1916, very quietly and without publicity, Chaplin tried to enlist, and was turned down. President Wilson commented that his film *Shoulder Arms* accomplished more for national morale than all

the overt propaganda put together (all the more remarkable
in that the picture was not anti anything). In addition to his
fund-raising campaigns during the First World War, Chaplin
was among the first to promote the opening of a Second Front,
in 1942. In all, he did as much for this country as any entertainer before or since. The actual charge, of course, obtains from
Chaplin's refusal to become an American citizen. Americans,
who customarily retain their citizenship when they go to live
abroad, cannot bear the thought of someone's moving here
without cutting all home ties. If a foreigner manages to get
past Ellis Island and make good in the United States, he *must*
become a citizen; if he does not, then he is an ungrateful wretch.

A moment's reflection on Chaplin's enormous popularity,
from the beginning, makes it abundantly clear that he could
have succeeded anywhere in the world. France would have been
delighted to supply the beloved Charlot with a home, just as
Spain would have welcomed Carlos and Italy opened its doors
to Carlito. To the list, add England and Germany and any
country you choose. That he preferred to produce his films here
is a fact for which *we* should be grateful.

After all, like Ernest Hemingway, he might have gone elsewhere; and, also like Hemingway, who considered himself a
Cuban ("I don't want people to think of me as a Yankee"),
he might have renounced America at the first disapproving
rumble.

As for his much-vaunted lecheries, they should be his business and his alone. Errol Flynn, before his death, admittedly
devoted himself to "women, liquor and amusement," becoming
involved in paternity and rape suits with monotonous regularity; yet, perhaps because he did not add to these the affront

of genius, he was secretly admired and generally considered a lovable scalawag. Flynn, even when he was consorting with girls young enough to be his granddaughters, could do no wrong. Chaplin could do no right. He was criticized for divorcing his first wife, Mildred Harris, whom he married in September 1917, even though it was an impossible union. The young girl had been swept away by the famous artist, dreaming, naturally enough, of a life of endless parties and communal glamor. She was totally unable to cope with the introspective side of Chaplin, which manifested itself in prolonged states of depression, lonely walks, unheralded disappearances; certainly she could not understand that these were the incubation periods for the art that was to follow. Although Chaplin granted the girl a handsome settlement, the press took him to task. When, some years afterward, he became enchanted by Lita Grey, signed her for the lead in *The Gold Rush,* and married her, the gossip was that he was about to make a fool of himself. And so he did, if falling in love and falling out again is foolish, if reaching desperately for the unattainable is foolish, if making a mistake and trying, honorably, to rectify it is foolish. Chaplin the man was lonely. In those years of his greatest artistic energy, there was little for him to give personally; yet he needed to give and to receive. He might have had all the women he desired, but sex alone was not enough. Even though he knew it was impossible, he wanted—as he confessed later in *Monsieur Verdoux*—the happy married life of an ordinary person.

By her own consent, Lita Grey was removed from *The Gold Rush;* she was far too busy being Mrs. Chaplin to bother with the rigors of a career, which she'd never really desired. The marriage lasted three years and ended in divorce. Lita's mother

released a number of ugly stories to the newspapers, charging
Chaplin with behaving like a genius ("monster" was her
word), and he was pilloried anew by the press. By now it had
become fashionable to attack Chaplin. As the facts did not
supply much ammunition, new "facts" were invented. About
the time Chaplin was preparing to give *The Circus* to the
world, a story circulated to the effect that Hannah Chaplin had
been "forgotten" by her famous son and was living in abject
poverty. She was, in fact, living in Santa Monica, in a lovely
house which Chaplin had purchased for her; and if he did not
visit her often, it was because he could not stand to see the
condition into which her mind had fallen. A nurse and doctor
attended Hannah until the day she died, and when she spoke
to them of her son, she called him "the King of them all."

Chaplin's marriage with Paulette Goddard looked promising, but the young actress was too much of an individualist to
walk in Chaplin's shadow, and his ego was too raw to with-
stand her emerging personality. After eight years of effort, they
were divorced. The almost simultaneous appearance in his life
of Joan Barry and Oona O'Neill provided the gossip-mongers
with their favorite weapons, and they used them with such
vengeance that within a few months Chaplin's reputation was
beyond repair. Joan Barry was the sort of waif or gamin that
Chaplin loved to feature in his films. Unlike his characters,
however, Miss Barry was not all sweet innocence. Her eyes had
seen a great deal of the world and were quick to recognize a
good thing when it came around. She signed a contract with
Chaplin and also became his mistress. When he tired of her,
he asked her to leave. In such situations, sympathy is usually
equally divided; but Chaplin got all the blame. He was painted

as a Svengali who had used up yet another Trilby and was now tossing her out into the cold. Miss Barry left, as she'd been asked to do, but she returned with demands, which Chaplin would not grant, and threats, which he ignored. It may be that he was unwise in underestimating the power of a teen-age girl. The gamin broke into his house, leveled a pistol at him, insisted that he make love to her, then announced to the world at large that she was going to have a baby.

Public opinion was entirely against Chaplin in the ensuing trial, which included not only the paternity suit but also a charge of violation of the Mann Act. The latter was laughed out of court thanks to the skills of defense lawyer Jerry Giesler, but the paternity charge stuck—despite the statement of an accredited physician that the child could not possibly have been Chaplin's.

Now the creator of the Little Tramp was a bona fide villain. The experience might well have embittered him permanently but for his new-found friendship with Eugene O'Neill's lovely daughter, Oona. Though only eighteen years old, she was no stranger to the shapes of genius. Whether because of the relationship with her famous father, beside whom most artist-eccentrics might seem like Rotarians, or because of an inborn understanding, she knew how to deal with Chaplin's moods. And she loved him.

If the marriage itself was not enough to finish them both in America, its success was.

Chaplin made two more films here—the brilliant *Monsieur Verdoux* and *Limelight*—but they were not appreciated, and so he left us.

It is for these reasons, for his occasional weaknesses as a

person and for his incredible strengths as an artist, that Charles Chaplin became one of the most despised men in America. Now, in Vevey, Switzerland, he lives quietly with his wife and seven children—one of whom this remarkable man sired only recently, despite the fact that he is in his seventies. Because he is in his seventies, Chaplin will, before long, die. And then, because his legend has been all but destroyed, he will probably be forgotten, as most men are.

But what Chaplin created we must not allow to be forgotten: Charlie the fool. Charlie the clown. Charlie, the spirit of Man, walking with a goatlike skip of his oversize shoes and a hitch of his baggy pants—bewildered, but unafraid—into the unknown. Charlie, the best of us.

Tune in yesterday

THE PROBLEM, a typical one, was to turn a man inside out. Gordon Hughes, grand master of an art lost to us now, considered and rejected the obvious solutions. It had to be *authentic,* not merely convincing. Of course, it was a good bet that most people did not know what a man being turned inside out sounded like, but the wonder and the challenge of it was that they knew what a man being turned inside out did *not* sound like. Hughes and his fellow alchemists realized this odd fact. By the tedious process of trial and error they found that in order to express the whole they would have to separate the parts, as follows: (1) Flesh: a rubbery, snapping effect; (2) Bones: a grinding, crunching effect; and (3) Blood and Guts: a squishing effect. Thus categorized, the job became a matter of routine. For the first part of the problem, Flesh, they used a length of inner tube. A technician grasped the bottom of this device with his left hand, inserted his right arm into the tube, grasped the top section firmly, and yanked. Effect: a rubbery, snapping sound. For Blood and Guts, a tub of warm cooked spaghetti and two bathroom plungers sufficed. Problem Number Two, Bones, was somewhat more difficult. Various types of woods were tried, but with signal lack of success. Soda crackers crunched well enough, yet there was a certain feeling of depth still missing. One of the earnest artisans sardonically offered to sacrifice his left leg, but the gesture was refused on the grounds that the effect, though genuine, might, as was so often the case with "actual" noises, sound spurious; besides, it allowed no chance for rehearsal. Finally someone put a Lifesaver between his teeth, motioned for silence, stood close to the mike, and proceeded to grind the candy slowly into powder.

Combined, these three effects succeeded in turning the stomachs of all the *Lights Out* fans across the nation.

More stomachs are being turned today, but for different reasons. The Sound Effects man is gone. He who plunged knives into defenseless heads of cabbage; who wore a throat mike and chewed celery, thereby conjuring up a rogue elephant crashing through the jungle, splintering the bamboo saplings and tearing up the ground . . . along with the minstrel, the rainmaker, the marathon dancer, the giant roc, this man is a legendary figure from another time. Yet the time was hardly a generation ago, and many matured men of today, who did not gather to mourn his passing, wrote between the thin blue lines of their three-hole notebook paper: "What I Want To Be When I Grow Up—A Sound Effects Man."

Hardly a generation ago. Fins were on sharks then. A jet was what a woman's hair was as black as, in *Spicy Detective*. Rockets, missiles and atoms were strange and exotic words which cropped up occasionally in the *Buck Rogers* comic strip and in those new science-fiction magazines.

As for television, it was only a fanciful gimmick, exhibited at world's fairs along with the Westinghouse robot. And of the two, the robot seemed far the more practical.

It was not, I suppose, a better time then, in the thirties and forties, except as the time of one's awakening is better; but it was different. We were simpler. We were less sophisticated. There was war, but it was still an understandable sort of business, with villains and heroes and glorious deaths, and we were thrilled by it. We believed in individual triumph and individual failure. A person was either good or bad. The good, we felt, should be rewarded, and the bad punished. A few psychologists and philosophers and writers were beginning to hint that mankind was a mixture, that virtue and evil were only labels we pasted on complex emotional conditions, but we didn't believe the fancy words. Things had to be clear-cut for us. It is true that we weren't too smart. But, some of us having bungled our way to adulthood, we can say that there are certain rewards in being not too smart. Naïveté gave us things the kids don't have now. It gave us the magicians, those tall, dark men in black cloaks who smelled of sulphur and could whisk a rabbit into thin air or saw a woman completely in two, without ill effect; it gave us the carnivals and the smell of sawdust and the sound of strange men promising miracles for a quarter and the fearful gloom of tents filled with alligator women and men who could write their names with their toes; it gave us the earth-shaking, sleep-destroying, brain-exploding circuses, those vast enchanted worlds, forever gone, of elephants and clowns and aerialists and lion tamers and bareback riders and magic people in suits of jewels that sparkled long after the circus had moved on to delight the children of another town; it gave us men whose job it was to make the sound of a man being turned inside out.

It gave us radio.

They say that radio is alive and healthy, but they're wrong. Radio, as we knew it and loved it with all our young hearts and minds, is dead, and it could no more come back than could the magicians or the carnivals or the circuses. It is entombed with these remnants of a vanished era, not far from where the troubadours and minnesingers lie.

It is our business now to lay a friend to rest.

Imagine yourself thirteen summers young in a world that stretched as far as the eye could see, but no farther; a world of boring visits to ancient aunts and Sunday drives and triple features, plus serial and two cartoons, of baseball in the streets and zoos and jawbreakers and Indian gum and penmanship and firecrackers and Tarzan and the Scarecrow. It's morning. Off to the gray prison, school, and the heavy books, the ceramic women with their fiery eyes, and the clock-hands that never moved. One o'clock. A century later, two o'clock. Two centuries later, three o'clock. Saved by the bell! Out of your seat then, out the doors, down the steps, running, you and your friends, though never so fast you forgot to step on every third crack in the pavement, and, finally, home.

Maybe it was kick-the-can for you. Or over to Phillip's, or Jimmy's, or Fred's, for a peanut-butter-and-jelly sandwich. Or tag football. Whatever it was, the chances are you didn't stay at it very long. Around five, when the soft dark had begun to gather, somebody would say: "Whose house?" Somebody would answer "Mine!" and off you'd fly.

If your house was "it," you'd be the first to the radio. You were proud of that radio because it was almost as tall as you were and twice as heavy, and its dark polished wood reflected the light. While your friends squatted on the carpet, you turned the middle dial and waited for the hum and changed stations with the speed and accuracy of an engineer.

A hush.

Then, the call to adventure, the words that sent chills down your back every time you heard them: *"Jack Armstrong, the All-American Boy!"*

You set the volume just right, you scooted along the carpet until your head was directly underneath the radio, you closed your eyes, and you listened. . . .

After the most popular song in America ("Have you *tried* Wheaties? The best breakfast food in the land. Won't you *try* Wheaties? They're whole wheat with all of the bran!"), the rich, confidential voice of the announcer—omniscient, as all announcers were—bringing us up to date, as though any of us needed it:

Jack and Billy are rowing their hearts out—getting the last of the supplies aboard the two-masted schooner *Spindrift*. The *Spindrift* rides her mooring like a gray ghost while the San Francisco fog hides her from the view of hostile eyes on shore. The schooner is all ready to start on her perilous journey to the Sula Sea to recover a precious cargo of [this was back in the thirties, remember!] uranium, sunk off an uncharted reef. Jack and Billy, as they bend to the oars, know that other persons are trying desperately to get possession of a mysterious ring which Uncle Jim has just received —a ring which may contain the secret of the uranium. Betty, alone on the schooner in the fog, is having the fright of her life—but Jack doesn't know it—yet! *Listen!*

Listen we did. After drifting for twelve minutes in a fog-bound sea, we leapt up, sent away two boxtops and ten cents in coin or stamps for an exact replica of Uncle Jim's mysterious ring, and scooted back barely in time to switch from schooner to sampan. Terry was engaged in a week-long duel with the Pirates, and things were not going well.

He was having a picnic, though, compared to Captaaiiinnnn Midnight, whose single-engine plane just ran out of gas over the Himalayas.

Still, of them all, it may have been that the Lone Ranger was in the worst shape. In a gallant effort to rescue his faithful friend Tonto, the Masked Man found himself, along with a dozen kegs of dynamite, locked in a burning cabin.

The world of radio was real to us. There are squirts and small fry today who will soon be as old as the Us of Then, and I know some who haven't turned a radio on in their entire lives. I try to tell them what it was like, but they don't understand. They can't believe I'm talking about the little plastic box in the kitchen that plays rock-'n'-roll songs and gives us the news, and I'm not sure I believe it, either. Television is the substitute for what we had, and I deem it a bad one. It inspires neither loyalty nor awe. It does not thrill, transport, terrify or enchant. It only entertains. The kids, as a rule, can take it or leave it alone.

Of course, ninety-nine percent of the shows on TV are trash; but I don't think this is the reason for our generally dispassionate reaction. Research into the subject shows that most of the quality we now associate with radio did not exist. We think the material was top drawer, but we are only trying to justify our profound nostalgia: the truth is that radio offered very little in the way of quality. Whereas television has developed such fine writers as Paddy Chayefsky, Rod Serling, Reginald Rose, Tad Mosel, James Costigan, Horton Foote, and at least a dozen others; an imposing roster of actors and directors; and such excellent dramatic programs as *Hallmark Hall of Fame, Playhouse 90, Studio One* and *Alcoa-Goodyear Playhouse,* radio in all its years could boast but two consistently first-rate dramatic writers—Norman Corwin and Arch Oboler—and a handful of really adult shows.

The reason probably lies in the essential difference between the two media. Television makes no demands, except upon our patience. It presents its stories ready to wear. All the work is done. There is nothing we can contribute. For this reason, television is an impersonal form of entertainment. Radio was something else again. What was originally thought to be its greatest limitation, lack of visual interest, turned out to be its greatest strength. It made a direct appeal to what producer-writer Blake Edwards calls "the great ally, imagination." Through the use of sound effects, music, a very special form of writing, and acting which bore scant relationship to other modes of acting, radio created a world which had to be believed to be seen. Participation was not merely desirable; it was essential. Radio provided a sketch, but it was up to the listener to make the finished picture. The greater reality was his to create. Thus programs were real or unreal depending entirely upon the imagination quotient of the participant. Radio can be said therefore to have been a personal medium.

It was closer to narrative than to drama. As with narrative it had no location or set problems, and casting was always perfect. If a script called for "a city of golden towers, stretching to infinity," the city was built. Not by stagehands, nor by studio carpenters, but by a few words and a little music. A woman described as "the loveliest creature in the world" was exactly that. When Sam Small flew, he really and truly *flew*, without the aid of piano wire or trick photography. When the *Lone Ranger* announcer, in his standard opening, spoke of "A fiery horse with the speed of light," we saw—metaphorical miracle! —exactly that. Nothing was impossible in the world of radio. It was a wild, illogical world, but it made perfect sense to us kids. We were never bothered by the fact that time did not exist as it did in the "actual" world. A minute could last a week, a month could go by in a matter of seconds, yet we were not concerned. Even when they turned time backward, to let us know what Kato was doing when the Green Hornet walked into that trap, we accepted it, presumably on the theory that if it was happening, it was happening. We radio listeners were able to accommodate two separate and distinct truths. We believed that Doc, in *I Love a Mystery,* was an actor and we believed that he was Doc. So it was that when an unknown actor replaced Barton Yarborough in the central role, we wrote heated letters to the network, advising whom it might concern that the wool hadn't been pulled over our eyes, or ears, and to Jack and Reggie warning them that an impostor had taken Doc's place and that they'd better watch out.

We were an extraordinary audience. Perpetually accused by our parents of "not concentrating," I think we must have been the greatest concentrators of all time. In a single evening we would travel up the Yangtze, fight ravenous wolves in the frozen wastes of the Yukon, ascend into the stratosphere in a leaking balloon, skim the bottom of the Atlantic Ocean, shoot it out with desperadoes in a Chicago alley, cut down a dozen pirates, get trapped by an avalanche, and sink into a coma as the result of having been pierced by a dart tipped with deadly curare; yet we kept our heads. Some of us even managed to do our homework at the same time. I can think of no period during those years when we did not have at least twenty different stories and a hundred or so characters to carry around in our brains, and I can think of no one who ever lost track. We might forget the principal products of Bolivia, or the date of the Magna Charta, but when it came to our radio heroes, the latest IBM machine should have such a memory.

Although we realized vaguely that somebody wrote the shows we loved and somebody produced and directed them and a lot of actors and actresses acted in them, we were an incurious lot. It may be that we were aware of the delicate balance of our beliefs, and how easily that balance could be upset. Each of us had his own conception of, say, Lamont Cranston, otherwise known as the Shadow. For me, he was about six feet two, ruggedly handsome, dark-haired, and impeccable in matters of dress. For you, he may have been on the short side, somewhat chubby, blond and casual. It doesn't matter; we were both right. So long as we never saw a picture of him, that is. Unfortunately, the networks did not fully understand this. From time to time they would release photographs of the actors, and we were invariably disappointed. I could be wrong, but it seems that the heroes of our dreams always turned out to be suspicious little men with pencil mustaches and bad teeth. Eventually the networks realized that they were like the magicians who enchant you and then insist upon showing you how it wasn't enchantment at all but simply sleight of hand, and the men behind the scenes returned to their anonymity.

But it has been years now since the last magician passed through town. The shows we loved were considered trivial. No one bothered to record them, practically all the scripts were destroyed, and so they are gone—which is to say, they can never be taken from us now. "If you want your castle to last, build it of sand," says Walter Kerr, and he's right. The enchanted hours are locked away in our minds. No one can get to them now except us. So it will not hurt, I think, in this requiem, to call a roll and look at the men and women who created and sustained for so many years our dear dead friend.

The first radio program was a disc jockey show: records and gab. Emanating from Brant Rock, Massachusetts, on the eve of Christmas, in the year 1906, it was heard by wireless operators on all ships within a three-hundred-mile radius. Over twenty years passed before the dramas began, but when they came in, they came in strong. The writing was of a necessarily specialized nature, and because of this, few established authors were able to make the transition. They had too much to unlearn. For this reason, those who succeeded got their start as engineers or ad men or station owners.

Of course, there were exceptions. Notable among these was Archibald MacLeish, whose verse-play *The Fall of the City* won just about every available prize and stands as the high point in radio drama. Norman Corwin brought quality to the airwaves, though in retrospect his orotund antiwar messages seem more valuable as propaganda than as art. Still, it was he who defined and shaped strict radio style, and through his influence the classic form was developed. Corwin demonstrated the vast potential of radio drama by abolishing both time and space. He created the little musical bridges that spanned centuries, and helped to create most of the other technical magics. If anyone deserves the title Mr. Radio, it is surely he. Equally an innovator, but slightly less a pure talent, was horror-specialist Arch Oboler. Oboler wrote the way a machine gun fires. A script a day was routine, but occasionally he would do two or three, and once in a while even four within a twenty-four-hour period. They were all short on characterization, as might be expected, but a surprising number of them showed real imagination. Oboler's *Lights Out* dramas, in particular, were rich in the stuff of horror. One week he would give us a story about an experiment on a chicken's heart which causes the heart to grow and grow until it covers the earth (at the end of this play, the last survivors are cruising at six thousand feet in their private plane; we hear the drone of the single engine; then the dry cough and spluttering which indicate that the plane is running out of gas; another cough, a final splutter, a rush of air, a ghastly SPLOOGE! as the machine is swallowed up, and then the steady, horrible THOOMP-THOOMP of the earth-encompassing heart). The following week, he would give us a woman who turns into a cat and eats her favorite canary; the week after that, a variation on the chicken-heart yarn—a hole in the ground that gets deeper and wider and deeper, until . . . It

wasn't art, but it was effective, and it had magic. Oboler's intention was to scare us silly, and silly he scared us.

Of course, the child psychologists objected to the plethora
of horror on radio, but as a matter of strict and demonstrable
fact, most shows were very moral. At the end of each episode
we were reminded that although the villains appeared to be
having a grand time, they would inevitably be crushed under
the humdrum heel of Good. Or, as the Shadow so aptly put
it: "The weed of crime bears bitter fruit." And *he* knew.

There were even more subtle appeals to the moral sense.
Breathes there a man among us who does not remember vividly
the Elephants' Graveyard chapter in *Jack Armstrong?* Elephants, we learned, were wise and mysterious animals who
knew when they were about to die. It mattered not whether
from disease, a wound (barring direct brain shots), or old age:
they knew; and, feeling the bitter wind from The Great
Scythesman upon them, they would lumber proudly to a secret
place and lay their heavy living cargo down and quietly die.
In a fog-shrouded valley hidden deep in the deepest part of
unknown Africa were ten thousand elephant skeletons and
twenty thousand ivory tusks. It was a great white cathedral,
holy and untouched. To disturb it would be sacrilege. Ivory we
knew to be valuable, and so it was no surprise to learn that
there were certain unscrupulous men, evil to the last whisker
of their black beards, who had so little regard for what was
proper that they actually intended to pillage the cemetery—and
for the basest reason of all: money. It took Jack a long time
(something like six months) to thwart the monsters, but he
succeeded, and we all rejoiced. A child today might ask why.

The men were only trying to turn a little profit on some dead bones, after all, weren't they? *No!* They were trying to defile beauty, ruin loveliness, flout tradition. Not a bad message, it seems to me.

Then of course there were the prizes. We can't talk about radio without mentioning the wonderful things that kids got for two boxtops and coin-or-stamps. Among the more memorable treasures:

Rings. With secret compartment (for hidden messages); with decoder (for clues regarding next week's adventure); with siren (for summoning aid); with identification (for showing your friends that you were a member in good standing of the Secret Squadron); with compass (for never getting lost); and with mirror (for checking to see that you were not being followed). All bright as quicksilver upon arrival, these items were guaranteed to turn your finger dark green in a week. *Badges.* With cluster leaf for spirit of faith shown by sending extra boxtops. *Periscopes.* For seeing around fences and spying on your enemies. *Hike-O-Meters.* For measuring how far you walked in a day. *Ovaltine shakers.* For holding next to your forehead when dissolved Ovaltine crystals and milk had turned the shaker cold and frosty. *Charms. Buttons. Wings. Silent Whistles.* And a hundred other precious gewgaws, eagerly awaited and delightedly received by small fry who didn't know or care that they were making the manufacturers rich.

I think of my childhood friend, radio, and I wish I could go back to him for a little while. For an hour. One hour with my eyes closed and my mind open, lying on my back under those great carved wooden legs, listening. Listening to the kid

shows, but to many of the grown-up shows too; listening and
listening and listening . . .

To *Little Orphan Annie* ("Who's that little chatterbox, the
one with pretty auburn locks?"); *Don Winslow of the Navy*
("Oh, Cuh-*lumm*-byuh the Gem *uv* the Oh-shunnn!"); *Buck
Rogers* (". . . in the Twenty-Fifth CENNNN-tureeee!"); *The
Lone Ranger* ("A cloud of dust and a hearty Hi-yo Silverrrr!
Awa-a-a-ay!"); *First Nighter* ("The little theatre off Times
Square"); *Vic and Sade* ("The little house halfway up in the
next block"); *Amos and Andy* ("Buzz me, Miss Blue"); *Gang
Busters* ("Rat-tat-tat-tat-tat-tat!"); *Og, Son of Fire; Terry and
the Pirates; Captain Midnight; The Green Hornet; Wilderness
Road; King of the Royal Mounted; The Shadow; Peter Quill;
Lights Out; Inner Sanctum; The Hermit's Cave; The Molle
Mystery Theatre; Suspense; Mr. Keene, Tracer of Lost Persons;
Columbia Workshop; Theatre Guild on the Air; Lux Radio
Theatre; John Nesbitt's Passing Parade* . . . and the Metro-
politan Opera and the New York Philharmonic . . . Edgar
Bergen and Charlie McCarthy, Kate Smith, Jack Benny, Don
Wilson, Harry von Zell, Fred Allen, Fibber McGee and Molly,
Nelson Olmsted, Paul Rhymer, and George Hicks, speaking
to you *for* United States Steel. To Orson Welles and his Mer-
cury Players, who convinced us that the Martians had arrived.
To Nila Mack and the *Let's Pretend* people, who filled our lives
with beauty. To Raymond, Your Host, and Arch Oboler, and
Willis Cooper, who kept us shivering under the covers. To
James Fassett, who taught us that Mozart wrote some pretty
tunes. To Archibald MacLeish and Norman Corwin, who gave
us poetry and drama. Yes, and even to *Helen Trent* and *Life
Can Be Beautiful* and *The Goldbergs* and *Stella Dallas* (plus

Stella's nemesis, "the wealthy *but insane* Ada Dexter") and the Story That Asked the Question: Can a girl from a little mining town in the West find happiness as the wife of a wealthy and titled Englishman?

But—sadly—I *can't* go back. So: to all the terrible, wonderful shows, all the lost hours of enchantment, all the laughter and fear and dreaming—a salute, and a farewell.

And a glass
of water, please

THEY ARE not gone yet, but they're going: the drugstore soda fountains of yesterday, where a guy could clamber up on a wire-legged stool and brood away an hour or more. They were fine for brooding. They were also fine for exulting, dreaming, wondering, and plotting revenge. And they were magnificent for eating and drinking. The food wasn't fancy, but that was all right, because the drinks and the treats were. With a ham sandwich, or a burger, as the base, one could order from an almost infinite variety of treats. If you felt expansive, and had some allowance left, or had managed to filch a bit from the old man's trousers last night, you could order a banana split. Watching the soda jerk build this temple of ice cream (vanilla, chocolate and strawberry), flavored syrup, fresh (not canned) peaches, sliced bananas, syrup again, whipped cream, crushed almonds and, topping it all, maraschino cherries, you knew that you were watching the creation of a work of art, and you were awed. Of course you wanted to eat it, for you knew it was the best, the most deli-cious banana split in all the world, but you hesitated. It was such a perfect thing. It shouldn't be spoiled by plunging spoons; it should be exhibited in a museum somewhere.

But then the soda jerk would slide it along the polished marble counter, and you would take up your spoon, because, after all, the man would be insulted if you didn't at least taste his creation. He would grin, for reasons you didn't understand, and you would grin back, and you would begin. You would eat the cherries first, then a bit of the chocolate ice cream, some of the strawberry, a smidgin of rare banana, some more choco-late, a soupçon of nuts and syrup, and, eventually, years later, you would finish. The canoe-shaped dish would be empty now, gleaming with memories, like your eyes. And you would be content.

The next day you would make do with a phosphate. These came in a polychromatic variety, and you felt, perhaps correctly, that you could order a different flavor every afternoon and never taste all of them.

Each drugstore had its own specialty then, upon which copyright no other drugstore infringed. It would have been considered unsporting. So if you were in the mood for a Green River Float Deluxe, you could go to the place on the corner, where the decoction was originally created, whereas it would require a walk of four blocks if you preferred an Iron Brew Fizzie. Green River and Iron Brew could be taken neat, par-ticularly the latter, whose bottlecap design—a hugely muscled arm snapping a chain—suggested that you were improving your physique as you quenched your thirst; but they were more often used as the mix for exotic cocktails.

Who doubts that they were exotic has forgotten that they were prepared by master pharmacists. Some of the bigger places could afford unskilled labor, but the authentic or neighborhood drugstores tolerated children on one side of the counter only. The art of mixing an all-chocolate double-scoop soda was not taken lightly. As with anything else, there was a right way and a wrong way of doing it. Done right it could be a treat for the gods; done wrong, a gooey mess. If one had integrity, one simply did not entrust such arcane matters to pimply school-kids.

There was something exciting, too, about the knowledge that the man who was mixing your strawberry malt had probably just finished mixing a batch of weed killer. You wondered how it was that he never made a mistake. Secretly, you hoped someday he would. You could see him standing there by the mortar, a pestle in one hand, a phial of strychnine in the other. The phone rings. He answers it, still holding the strychnine. Then he sees someone (your neighborhood tormentor) at the counter. He sets the bottle down next to the flavored syrups. A cherry phosphate is ordered. He reaches for the cherry syrup, grabs the strychnine by mistake . . .

It was a lovely thought. Somehow you knew it wouldn't happen, but it could, it could, and you only hoped you'd be around to watch the dirty rat (your tormentor) suffer.

Now, in this age of specialization, the cobbler is sticking to his last, and the pharmacist to his pharmaceuticals, and this may be why the drugstore soda fountain, as we knew it, is disappearing. Everywhere, except in the big places, which are themselves divided into specialized categories offering everything from ceramic ducks to recordings of *The Goldberg Vari-*

ations, the sign FOUNTAIN CLOSED flourishes. Where it does not, it should. For the drugstore Renaissance man has perished, and with him his masterpieces.

You can still buy banana splits, but they are like dime-store prints of great paintings, whereas in our day each was an original. Partly it is because one outgrows one's taste for certain things (whoever dreamed he would tire of the Sunday funnies?). Partly it is because the soda jerks of today are inept fumblers, taking little, if any, pride in their jobs. I doubt that any boys of this generation dream of growing up to be soda jerks. It is considered a demeaning position, slightly above that of dishwasher, and since it is at best a temporary situation, of course there is little point in becoming adept at it. Enough to slop the stuff together and get it on the counter without spilling too much.

Understandable. Perhaps the *chefs des glaces* of yesterday would have behaved the same if this had been their only occupation. But it wasn't. They could afford, not through an excess of money but through a sufficiency of pride, to perfect their skills. If someone had suggested that they could save time and money by using vertical glasses for banana splits, by chopping up the bananas instead of slicing them with mathematical precision, they'd have thought that someone was crazy.

And they'd have been right.

Don't miss

the next

thrilling chapter!

IN A review of Ian Fleming's thriller, *Goldfinger,* a critic commented that for him the book was "the most fun since movies came in chapters." A generation nurtured by the regurgitants of television and Double-Monstro-Scope will doubtless miss the allusion, but to codgers of twenty-five, or more, that casual phrase contains the stuff of dreams, the newly-opened-crypt aroma of which one whiff is sufficient to set the nostalgia glands fibrillating. For movies did come in chapters, once upon a simple, long-ago time, and they were loved by the young fry of America as few things are ever loved. The Serials! An institution in their heyday; in their decline, a national addiction, comparable in importance to Donald Duck cartoons, Indian gum, traveling carnivals, Big Little books, Petty drawings, Edgar Rice Burroughs, and the Land of Oz, mainlined every Saturday afternoon by all the howling, shrieking, giggling, gawking, popcorn-pop-and-jujube-filled creatures that were this country's youth and are, today, this

country's sober, graying, gaunt adults. It would be impossible
for children now to visualize their fathers (the addiction wasn't
wholly for males; one seems to recall the faintly embarrassing
and embarrassed hysteria of girls in the darkness; still, it was
mostly for males) clad in beanies, cords and regimentally tattered T-shirts, picking streamers of cotton from theatre seats,
hurling fat flowers of popcorn up into the mysterious widening
shaft of light and watching the popcorn blaze into flecks of
silver fire, blowing just so into empty pop bottles and making
a sound like foghorns or ocean liners lost in the night, then
falling into silence at the end of "The Eyes and Ears of the
World," detonating and exploding at the announcement of
the serial, and hushing again, the theatre still, as still as the
dark side of the moon, except for the vast collective inrush of
breath, the licking of lips and pounding of small hearts, and
the few muted whispers of "He'll get out okay" and "How
can he? The rope broke and he was falling headfirst right
into the goddam acid, for crying out loud!" and "Shut up, you
guys, it's started already!"—yet, it is so. The man at the bank
who shakes his head, sighs and says no, he couldn't possibly
issue a loan without adequate collateral, was one of those creatures. The man who says, "Baby, are you awake? Listen, I
don't know what we're going to do. It can't go on this way,
it just can't. Helen has found out about us," is what's become
of the creature who snorted "Love stuff!" and bolted out into
the lobby for some Milk Duds and a licorice whip and bolted
back just as the kissing stopped. And the man who says,
". . . eight; seven; six; five; four; three; two; one; zero"
walked out into the blinding sunlight, not so very many years
ago, idyllically happy that Flash and Dale had managed to

get their rocket ship off the ground before Ming the Merciless could catch them and feed them to the Lizard Men.

Of course, those ex-kids would have had an equally difficult time visualizing their fathers before them reacting with equal vigor to the silent absurdities of the pre-twenties; yet that, too, was so. People—most especially young people—loved the serials from their birth, in 1913, to their death, in 1956.

Were they good pictures, so to infect two sprawling generations? Certainly not. By every adult standard, they were, as one critic commented in *Films in Review,* "ghastly illiteracies." But by another standard, the serials were magnificent. The basic requirements of drama were almost invariably met, in that sympathetic people were constantly involved in conflict toward the attainment of a goal. And the highest aim of all, the one striven for by dramaturgists since Aristophanes—audience empathy—was achieved almost casually by the unsung impresarios of this vanished American art-form, who successfully yanked millions of young patrons out of their cracked-leather and frayed-velvet seats every week end and hurled them into the wild and improbable worlds of the back lot.

"Ghastly illiteracies" may be accurate, but it is unkind. For what other adjuncts of our spare time, after-school existence, barring radio adventure plays and an occasional freshly minted comic book, can we hark back to with such unalloyed pleasure? Prior to our discovery of girls, which was either the beginning of the end or the end of the beginning, depending upon how one feels about it, what, indeed, can be recalled with anything like the vividness of our memories of, say, *The Phantom Creeps* or *Flash Gordon Conquers the Universe?*

We enjoyed so-called "good" movies, too, but we knew that they were not for us. They were for that other race, the Adults. We would watch the moving shadows of Janet Gaynor, Fredric March and Adolphe Menjou in *A Star Is Born* or Rosalind Russell and Joan Crawford in *The Women,* but somehow they always remained shadows, flickering images of grown-ups involved in problems too remote for us to grasp or care about; whereas the problems of Tim Tyler, Prince Barin, Tailspin Tommy, or Secret Agent X-9 were real, believable, urgent and full of good sense. Instinctively we knew that the serials were for us, but this is not to say we considered them "kid-stuff." Far from it. Because we were contemptuous of everything we couldn't understand, and because we could understand the serials very well, our conclusion was that the serials were the only truthful and important films being made.

Annoyingly, there were some adults who insisted upon muscling in on our territory. Fathers would occasionally show up at the Saturday afternoon bedlam, on the excuse that somebody had to keep Junior out of trouble, and one's recollection is that these intruders appeared to have as much fun as anyone else. Which struck us as peculiar, for since we didn't care for their world, why should they care for ours? What right had they to meddle in business that didn't in any sense concern them?

What we didn't realize was that these were Serial devotees who had failed to outgrow their enthusiasm. One such man in our block, a dour and corpulent butcher named Matsinger, used to close up shop every Friday, in the face of dire threats from customers waiting to buy pork loin, because he didn't want to miss the latest installment of *The Clutching Hand.*

And why not? Serials were invented for the adult trade. It wasn't until the late nineteen thirties, when comic strip characters began to play principal roles, that producers took to aiming specifically at the juvenile market. And, according to spokesmen of the earlier generation, that is when serials became pale, emasculated copies of the great epics of *their* day.

The Serial had its Elizabethan days [says Edmond Hamilton, whose science-fiction adventure tales have delighted young readers for thirty years]. [It had] its thundering Marlowes and Websters, but the glow . . . faded. They made a robust and lusty art form into a tame insipidity. . . . I count myself fortunate that my own boyhood lay in those days before World War I which marked the peak of the terror serial. In that time, censorship was scattered and stumbling. Child psychologists had not yet arisen to worry parent-teacher associations about the influence of the films on their young. The general theory was that if a child was in a moving picture theatre, he was out of trouble. . . . The result was that the childhood of America was subjected to such a barrage of horrors as was never seen before nor since. Murder, arson, torture, drug addiction, white slavery and every other major crime were discharged upon our innocent minds week after week. And we loved it, and came back for more. . . .

There were Serials that were Serials, says Hamilton, who regards the loves of our own youth as "debasements." Certainly the titles would tend to support his view: *The Perils of Pauline, The Exploits of Elaine, The Lightning Raider, The Black Secret, The Phantom Foe, The Yellow Arm, Avenging Arrow, Do or Die, Haunted Valley, The Man Without a Face* —"each title good for fifteen to twenty injections of pure terror, right into the bloodstream."

Despite our memories, we seem to have missed the Golden Years. Or did we?

It is common knowledge that the first serial was *What Happened to Mary?*, produced by Edison in 1912. Unfortunately for historians, that common knowledge is wrong. "Mary" was not a serial at all, but rather a collection, or anthology, of short films, each a complete story.

The first real serial—that is, continuous story told in chapters or installments—was *The Adventures of Kathlyn,* which made its debut in Chicago in 1913. It starred Kathlyn Williams, a blonde of the sort usually described as statuesque, and its locale was India—not, to be sure, the real place, but the India of a scenarist's naive and fevered imagination. This group of three-reelers (given no generic title whatever) was shown in conjunction with a continuing fiction piece of the same title which was running in the Chicago *Tribune* as part of a circulation booster. The delectable Kathlyn was something of a cipher, in both the written and filmed stories, but her father had eccentricities enough for both of them. Among other hobbies, he collected wild animals, which, owing to a good heart, he permitted free access to the house and grounds. Kathlyn was threatened periodically by two horrors: the four-legged beasts, for whom she did not share Pater's fondness, and a despicable two-legged beast named Umballa. Umballa was a "Hindu rajah" who, for some twelve or fifteen episodes, alternately tried to force his odious attentions upon Kathlyn and feed her to the lions. In neither enterprise was he successful, owing to the almost clairvoyant intervention of the hero—

played by Thomas Santschi, who later attained screen fame for the great fist-fight in the original *The Spoilers*.

We went to it [says Hamilton], believing it was another three-reel feature. I can still remember the terrific emotional shock that came when Kathlyn was dumped into the lion-pit of the rajah's private Colosseum. The hero had sagaciously planted dynamite under the pit the night before. His intention was to blow up the lions, but his detonator wires failed to function. Desperately he leaped down into the pit. And then a bland sub-title advised us, "Come to See the Next Episode!"

Kathlyn being a fortnightly affair, the suspense between episodes was painfully prolonged. Those who had caught the first part stampeded to the theatre to catch the second, and the Hollywood Powers realized that they were onto a good thing.

The Perils of Pauline reduced the strain of suspense by appearing every week. Its title has survived in the popular memory as a prototype of the early serial, but aficionados claim that *Pauline* was neither the first nor the greatest of them. It did, however, set the pattern for the terror serial by demonstrating that masked murderers and sinister Chinese were more fearsome than any number of lions. Also, *Pauline* had the honor of launching the incomparable Pearl White on her long and hazardous career. It seems odd to us Flash Gordonites that all the early serials had female stars, but that is explained by the fact that the girl was simply the key to the plot. She always possessed a valuable secret and the villain was always out to get the secret (called "the weenie" by Miss White) by means foul and fearsome, inevitably thwarted, of course, by the hero. And Miss White, with her cloud of golden hair, her wide, terrified eyes and perpetually startled expression, was perfect as the menaced heroine.

Then, too, girls were different in those days. The lengths to which they would go to avoid the Fate Worse Than Death in any of its forms, persuades one that they didn't go for the Love Stuff any more than did our remembered stalwarts. Of course, their attitudes might have been different toward the heroes, but there was never any time to find out. They were always too busy being blown up in dynamited yachts, shackled to railroad tracks, stranded in captive balloons 250 feet over jagged precipices, locked in rooms whose walls close inexorably, or bound and gagged in Chinese opium dens ready for barter in the white slave traffic. In short, the girls in those days were real men.

George B. Seitz, the Dalai Lama of the serial creators, kept the redoubtable Pearl bouncing about like a ping-pong ball in numerous serials, of which at least one ran to thirty-six chapters. ("Action was the plot," commented Seitz. "The heroine had something the villains wanted. That was it.") So great was their popularity that Miss White was able to retire with a personal fortune of two million sound, 100-cents-to-the-buck U.S. dollars after nine years of cliff-hanging. She emigrated to Paris and there achieved additional fame for her lavish parties and a stable of pure white Hispano-Suiza automobiles.

But popular as the Pauline adventures were, it was the follow-up that really marked the full maturity of the terror serial. That was the "Elaine" series, a massive trilogy consisting of three serials: *The Exploits of Elaine, The New Exploits of Elaine* and *The Romance of Elaine.* These got such a grasp on youthful imaginations as to become an obsession.

Pearl White was again the star, and the hero was Arnold Daly, distinguished actor in Shaw dramas who had somehow strayed to this un-Shavian branch of the theatre. He played Craig Kennedy, the scientific detective. The villain was known as the Clutching Hand. He was a masked figure, wearing the attire of a thug and with one clawlike hand always ominously grasping the empty air. The great mystery of the first serial was the identity of the Clutching Hand.

Ed Hamilton remembers that there were five main characters.

. . . and since four of them were actively engaged in combating the masked terror, it seems that we might have suspected that the fifth was our man. We never did. I can still recall the terrific shock of astonishment that ran through juvenile circles when the final episode revealed that Perry Bennett, trusted family attorney of Elaine, was none other than the Clutching Hand.

That serial had been such a tremendous success that a sequel was necessary. The villain this time was Wu Fang, one of the gorgeous Chinese fiends of a day when international politeness was the film-makers' least worry. Wu Fang had proved his capacity for dirty work by double-crossing the Clutching Hand himself in the final scenes of the first serial. Now, for fifteen more episodes, his relentless attentions dragged Elaine through the doss houses and white slave marts of a highly sinister Chinatown.

The third serial of the trilogy came at a time when America was just entering World War I. That called for a change of villains. The opening scene is considered unforgettable by all those who saw it (and we must rely upon their memory, for no other trace of this masterpiece exists). It was in a lonely New England bay. A submarine rose from the depths, its conning-tower projecting ominously from the dark water. The hatch opened and from the submarine emerged Lionel Barrymore, a fiendish leer on his face. The Imperial German Government had sent him to America to "get" Elaine—for reasons no one recalls, except that she was dangerous. (That was one of Barrymore's first screen appearances. Although he mellowed subsequently into a gruff, grandfatherly type, he remained for many the archetype of evil he played in that initial adventure.)

It is widely thought that those early serials were "cheapies," but the fact is that they cost as much as regular high-class features: $90,000 to $125,000 apiece. Seitz once claimed that more care was actually taken in the matter of production—and no one could know this better than he. Seitz was called Mr. Serials, for the obvious reason that he was the most important single force in their production, with the possible exception of Frank Leon Smith. He wrote the second Pearl White thriller, later became a director and producer, and went on to create more than one hundred teeth-clenching, gut-wrenching, eyeball-popping serials, of which he wrote and acted in most. Setting the standard to which all successful serial men hewed, Seitz would never ask an actor to perform any stunt he wouldn't attempt himself. It is recorded that once he traded his clothes for the leading man's costume when that worthy balked at swimming an ice-encrusted river, leaped in, and wrapped up the day's shooting on schedule. Although he spent the twilight of a long and happy career directing the innocuous Andy Hardy series at M-G-M, Seitz gave serial drama its body and character by making the villains fiendish, the heroes larger than life, and the situations something you wouldn't wish on a blood enemy. He turned them into something very close to art.

Witness *The Iron Claw*. In this fearsome romp the villain (played by Sheldon Lewis, who had previously enacted the part of the Clutching Hand) was represented as having a hideous iron hook for one hand. It was the hero's identity that was secret this time. He was called the Laughing Mask, and whenever the Iron Claw had Pearl White backed against the ropes, the Laughing Mask infallibly showed up. In fact, he was so omnipresent that he apparently got the scenarist into a serious jam when the time came to expose him. The weak and wholly unsporting solution was that there were no less than a dozen Laughing Masks—which was the first of innumerable serial cheats, all of which were detected and mercilessly derided by audiences.

Pearl White, the heroine, and Warner ("Charlie Chan") Oland, the villain, were the great stars of the silent serials, but many celebrated "straight" actors were not above dabbling in the game. Warren William, Jack Mulhall, William Desmond, and Anna May Wong slashed, fought, menaced or added spice to various productions, while such non-acting personalities as Jack Dempsey, Gene Tunney, Red Grange and Harry Houdini were recruited from their professions to flesh out titles dreamed up by cubicle-bound writers.

The colorful Dempsey, having just knocked out Jesse Willard for the crown, was bound to be red hot "box office," so he agreed to punch his way through *Daredevil Jack* before going on tour with a circus to further exploit his fame. The serial was a great success, and led to the sort of gamble we know not in today's Ivy-league Hollywood. A producer signed Gene Tunney to a $3,000 per week contract just before his historic battle with Dempsey. The serial—called *The Fighting Marine* —was rushed to completion so that its release date would coincide with the big fight. If Tunney should win, the studio would score a fabulous scoop; if he should lose, as seemed likely—well, that was Show Biz! As we know, the scholarly pugilist did win, and *The Fighting Marine* cleaned up in the theatres as its leading man had done in the ring.

That peculiarly tragic figure, Houdini, conceded to be the greatest escape artist who ever lived, starred in a "Super Serial" called *The Master Mystery*. It may not have been the best serial ever made, but connoisseurs of the period agree that it is notable for its imaginative use of "P.T." (or Physical Threat).

In the first episode of *The Master Mystery,* a typically unique villain, the fiendishly clever mechanical man known only as the Automaton, and his subservient human gang, discover that Quentin Locke (Houdini) is a secret agent working to expose a ring of industrialists who are buying patents and keeping certain inventions off the market. (A "water motor" is mentioned as one of the devices.) Now this would seem like sound business practice today, but at the time the news was full of antitrust and monopoly prosecutions; so the industrialists were heavies. After administering an "almost unknown Oriental poison, *Dhatura Stramonium,*" to a defecting member of the ring, whose house Locke is bugging with a "strange listening device, called a *Dictagraph,*" the Automaton sets out to get rid of the snooper and wreak some kind of unspecified horror upon the heroine, Eva. Eva is, naturally, in love with the Federal man, Locke, and hates her fiancé, who is consort-ing with a thinly disguised prostitute named De Luxe Dora.

The Automaton's first attempt is foiled when Locke es-capes from a strait jacket, but he exacts sweet revenge by truss-ing up the nosy Fed by the thumbs and leaving him, several inches off the floor, to die. In a succeeding reel, the villain's men shackle Locke with handcuffs, leg irons and chains, then dump him into the Hudson River. Finding, to their amaze-ment, that this tactic is unsuccessful, they repeat the shackling job but take the added precaution of enclosing the battered hero in a packing crate (into which a hole has been thought-fully bored to admit water) before consigning him to the swirling river once again.

Using nearly all his talents this time, Locke escapes and re-appears, only to be forced into a sitting position in an electric chair. As shockproof as he is unchainable, Houdini eludes the fatal jolt but stays alive merely to fall victim to one of the most hideous assaults on human dignity ever devised.

Near the mansion owned by the paralyzed poison victim, there is an old acid factory whose vats still contain a potent residue of the corrosive liquid. Capturing the agent once more, the thugs bind him with rope and suspend him from a rafter above one of the huge tubs. The free end of the rope is care-fully secured by closing it in the crack of a door. Then, the villains, at the bidding of their steel-riveted superior, inform Eva of Locke's whereabouts—knowing full well that she will rush to the acid factory, throw open the door, thus releasing the rope, and, by her own hands, send her lover to his death in the seething fluid.

The term "cliff hanger" scarcely paints an adequate picture of a situation such as this.

Needless to say, the escape artist was not plunged into the acid vat and followers of this epic were permitted to writhe with him while the Automaton's bloodthirsty emissaries delivered a ticking bomb into his hands; sent rivulets of acid trickling across a stone floor where he lay bound with *barbed wire;* directed an elevator to the bottom of its shaft to crush him; and twisted the noose of a powerful mechanical garrote around his neck.

In between these industrious attempts on his person, Locke is periodically wrapped in netting or otherwise restrained while the Automaton moves toward Eva. She is sustained through all the maneuvers by her efforts to find an antidote for the "Madagascan Madness," brought on by the aforementioned "almost unknown Oriental poison," which has incapacitated her father. Suffering only slightly fewer terrors than Locke, she seems to be in constant flight from the Automaton, his personal gang, her fiancé (really the mastermind), or assorted outside thugs who are brought in on piecework. The latter includes as mangy a group of alleged Orientals as one would ever care to meet in Reddest China, who operate a thriving opium den as a sideline to recruiting for the white slave trade.

By 1918, the success of the serials had multiplied them beyond count or recall. Dust and a few memories are all that survive of most of the adventures, but it is known that *The Diamond from the Sky* was among the great achievements in the genre. One of the longest (over thirty episodes, fifteen minutes per episode), this *Ben-Hur* of serials captivated the nation. In its first chapter, a Southern aristocrat is struck and stunned by a falling meteor. Upon investigation, the meteor is shown to contain a gigantic and invaluable diamond, and so we're off—to a porridge of intrigue and violence so thick and so fast that even those fans who saw every episode remember only that "a hell of a lot was going on, every minute."

In the competition at that time, every conceivable background was tried. There were the railroad serials of Helen Holmes, which emphasized P.T. rather than terror. Helen's great specialty was a leap from one moving train to another, no mean stunt considering the ankle-length skirts of the period. There were sea serials, such as *Neal of the Navy,* and submarine serials. *Secret of the Submarine* was quite popular, despite its somewhat monotonous plot. Every episode ended with the stricken sub sinking to watery doom, only to rise in the following episode, phoenixlike, by grace of some last-minute miracle.

It is odd to record that the Western serial was never a great success in the Silent years, and was not often tried. Perhaps the only really popular ones were those starring William Duncan, a splendidly muscled thespian who had left an association with Sandow to enter the films. Duncan's serials, *The Fighting Trail* and *Vengeance and the Woman,* were mostly laid in mountain country, and the usual scene was the side of a vertigo-inducing cliff. Duncan and his heroine, a comely but perennially worried-looking ingénue, were forever being tossed off the cliff to alight on a providential ledge, thence to scramble back to precarious and only too temporary safety.

But it was the straight terror serial that was the most popular and most fondly remembered. And the terror serial reached its finest flowering just before the War (Number 1) in *The Mysteries of Myra*. If the natural and human wasn't enough to scare you out of normal growth in those days, this legendary masterpiece should have got the job done.

Myra concerned the efforts of an organization of wizards called the *Black Brothers* to recover certain incriminating papers bequeathed to the heroine by her father, a former member of the Lodge. As a contemporary of the times says, "Dracula and Frankenstein of latter-day films were babes compared to the creatures that haunted this wonderful serial."

Myra, the daughter and legatee of the revealing documents, was attacked by ghosts, elementals, vampires, werewolves and revenants. Her fiancé, one Dr. Alden (referred to as an "Occult Scientist"), was hip, however, and he gave back as good as the evil brotherhood could send out. For fifteen hair-raising chapters he was kept so busy repelling legions of inhumans who menaced the hapless girl that only in the concluding scene could they find time to set a wedding date.

In one chapter the Grand Master raised a fire elemental and dispatched it to turn Myra's modest residence into a raging inferno. Dr. Alden countered by raising a water elemental and succeeded in dousing the flames, but not before much of the surrounding neighborhood had been laid waste. In another try, the brotherhood transformed themselves into trees and surrounded the house, hoping to snare Myra in the web of their branches.

The climactic chapters showed Dr. Alden's skill and resourcefulness to best advantage. The brotherhood, weary of the long and unsuccessful battle, joined their brains to create, from nothing, a huge, manlike monster who was instructed to go forth and destroy the girl. Inasmuch as the thing was a figment of the mind, ordinary weapons would prove harmless. In addition, Dr. Alden, being a single occultist ranged against many, could not hope to exert sufficient mental pressure to gain control of the creature. His answer was to build an ingenious and impressive machine which could tune in the spirit world and retrieve those who had passed into that realm. Setting the dials, he pressed the control and, shortly, Myra's late father stepped out of the cabinet. Alden's hope to extract secret, helpful information from him were dashed when the old man merely delivered a warning that they were in great danger and disappeared back into the mechanism. Dr. Alden frantically tried to tune him in again, but the wizards had jammed the wavelength. Suddenly, the Monster itself charged out of the device!

In the laboratory, the inhuman being quickly grasped Myra and was heading for Dr. Alden when that scientist switched on a hypnotism machine whose flickering lights and whirling rings soon brought it under control. Once hypnotized, the monster was easy prey to Alden's command that he return to the Wizards and destroy them collectively. Back into the cabinet and off to the lair of the Brotherhood went their own creation to carry out the annihilation.

Now considering that they were raised on such fare, it is difficult to understand our parents' objections to the relatively tame atrocities perpetrated in the serials to which our generation was devoted, but that seems to be the way with adults. They learn from everyone's experience except their own. Logically, and according to the widely accepted Wertham theory *(prolonged exposure to extreme violence in any form causes violent inclinations*) Mom and Dad should have had their tender minds blasted for life by the orgies of crime and horror they had been witnessing on the screen. Yet, despite fearful prognostications by psychologists, relatively few serial-addicts went on to become white slavers, perverts, murderers, or evil geniuses.

Still, pressures had begun to build during the Great Conflict, and Hollywood decided to cut down on the gore. Pearl White lingered on in a few chapter-plays, such as *Pearl of the Army,* and then abandoned the field. Her position as Queen of the Serials was filled by Ruth Roland, no less indefatigable than Miss White in dealing with criminals and terrors, but coming at a later and lesser day. The Roland serials—*The Red Circle, The Adventures of Ruth,* etc.—tended to avoid the exuberant horrors of earlier years. Comments Ed Hamilton: "The lurid heaven of our infancy was indeed fading into the light of common day. For a few years Ruth Roland, Ben Wilson, Eddie Polo and a few others maintained the great tradition, but by the mid-twenties the terror serial was practically dead."

What it evolved into is what most of us now remember. And though the serials of our generation may not have been touched with precisely the same wild-fire inspiration as those early *Meisterwerke* (I, for one, am not entirely prepared to accept the opinion as fact), they were enough to set our imaginations spinning.

Certainly the previous generation could not have been more devoted to their serials than we to ours. Saturday afternoon was Christmas, Thanksgiving, Halloween and the Fourth of July wrapped up into one glorious package, and it was delivered every week of the year. We woke up early in the morning, shifted about impatiently as the clock hands inched toward noon; then we bolted some Campbell's chicken soup, two glasses of milk, and a peanut-butter-and-jelly sandwich, rounded up the guys and went to the theatre—in the sense that the Goths "went to" Rome, which is to say that we advanced in a tattered army upon the theatre and then besieged it.

In our neighborhood picture palace, we were required to check our firearms at the box office before entering the auditorium. This we did willingly and with a peculiar sort of pride, perhaps because we would have been frisked in any case. Once inside, hidden by numbers and darkness, we raised a species of hell unknown to the comparatively orderly matinee-goers of today. In addition to an endless variety of mouth noises, we blew up popcorn bags and burst them (usually in accompaniment to some tender bit of dialogue on screen), rapped pop bottles against seat backs, dropped candy, cola, and other more substantial items from the balcony, and engaged in fisticuffs. No torment in any serial ever matched that of an usher (hated prison guard to us) or theatre manager (warden, also hated, but feared as well) during those unforgotten Saturdays.

The lobby photos advertising the current chapters went up, at our theatre, on Thursday, and we generally managed to stop by on the way home from school to try and figure out from these lurid stills what was in store for us. The game was interesting but highly unrewarding, since a goodly percentage of the pictures had nothing whatever to do with the action of the episode. But, instinctively understanding the come-on nature of the operation, we weren't resentful.

Not that we were incapable of resentment. Certain sins we

could not forgive, and of these one was cardinal. That was the sin of the phony resolution. They could never fool us, no matter how they tried. If we plainly saw the Hero at the reins of a runaway stagecoach as it careened over a mighty precipice into the river, we plainly saw it; and when on the following week we were asked to believe that the Hero really jumped off just before the coach shot into space, we howled and stormed and thundered our protest at the deception. If he had gone into the river and survived a fall that would have ended a lesser man, well, sure, we'd go along with that, but don't try to tell us we saw something we damn well knew we didn't see.

No mind is so quick to accept the impossible and reject the implausible as the mind of a pre-teen kid. We demanded logic within our illogical stories and insisted upon technical accuracy above all things. One classic boner which cost an otherwise good air serial its audience (or at least our segment of it) was one in which a tailspinning plane crashed behind a hill with a cataclysmic roar and burst of debris that clouded the screen. The following week's episode opened with a shot of the plane merely tipped up on its nose. The propeller wasn't even broken, and when the Hero's friend assisted him in restarting the engine and turning the craft around for a take-off, we shook the chandeliers with our disapproval and summoned a corps of flashlight-bearing ushers, who doubtless thought the theatre had exploded.

Another quality we insisted upon was consistency. We were ready to accept ray guns that slew or paralyzed and we embraced wholeheartedly the notion of lost planets, undiscovered continents, or subterranean civilizations, but if the bad guys and the hero were racing for a secret headquarters at the same time and the bad guys reached the spot first, we had damn well better be shown what delayed the hero. *Deus ex machina* did not go with us at all.

Of course there were minor irritations and tiny disillusionments, too. The inadequacy of the costumes always sort of upset us. This was no fault of the budget but merely the disadvantage of real life over art. In the comics, the skintight uniforms worn by many of the principals stayed skintight no matter what antics were performed. Unhappily, Batman's longies had a tendency to get baggy about the knees from time to time, and the Phantom's woolen outfit looked downright uncomfortable in the steaming subtropical heat of his African home.

But we had few complaints. The serials accounted for our richest moments, and we were certain that whoever was responsible for those glorious films had to be a genius.

If so, then Sam Katzman is the greatest genius Hollywood has ever known. For with the *Götterdämmerung* of the silent regime, Katzman took over as the foremost impresario of the episodic thriller, which position he held to the end.

Unlike Seitz, who considered himself something of an artist, Katzman approached serials with what may be described as a Good-Old-Fashioned-Yankee-Practical, or Get-the-Gold, attitude. Having served an apprenticeship at Columbia, where he gained a reputation as Master of the Quickie, it was only natural that he should apply his economic skills to this allied genre; and in no time at all, through the Katzman influence, serials became Big Business.

Though he was mostest with comic-strip characters, he was not fustest. In 1936 Universal produced *Flash Gordon,* based on Alex Raymond's popular creation. So successful was this serial that Katzman decided to use it as a model, and there followed a trend which continued through the life of serials.

But Katzman never managed to match his model. The Flash Gordon trilogy was the Elaine of our generation, remembered by the faithful as the absolute and unchallenged pinnacle of the form. All three serials starred the Olympic swimmer Larry "Buster" Crabbe as Flash, and a better choice for the role cannot be imagined. It is customary to think of the unfortunately-named Crabbe as a nonactor, but, having had a chance to review his performances on television reruns, I can happily report that he was every bit as good as we thought he was. Physically he was perfect, perhaps the only human being who really looked like a comic-strip character. His acting style was not bravura, true, but then the stories didn't call for that sort of thing, and we would have rejected it in any case. It was more than enough that he was sincere and athletic. And no one who ever saw him flare his nostrils could accuse him of unemotionalism.

It may even be that Buster Crabbe's nostrils were the greatest *shtick* any actor ever had. According to the degree and speed of distention, they could express anger, hatred, fear, annoyance, perturbation and lust. Lust pervaded the first *Flash,* by the way. The bowdlerized versions currently on display do not suggest the extent to which the producers went in spicing up their adventure. Dale Arden (played by Jean Rogers) was not the virtuous girl scout she subsequently became. Flash's nostrils told us, in no uncertain terms, that holding hands was not all this wench had on her mind. The scene in which she writhed, arms spread and shackled to the wall, attempting to avoid pattycake with the minions of Ming, gave many of us our first hint that perhaps there was more to sex than love stuff. And Priscilla Law, who played the evil, albeit beautiful, Allura, made us sure of it.

The second in the trilogy, *Flash Gordon Conquers the Universe,* took us away from the erogenous and into other, no less titillating, zones. Guided by Ray Taylor and serial director Ford Beebe, who had taken the reins from Fred Stephani, this chapter-play offered us further adventures on the planet Mongo, with Flash doing battle against the infamous Emperor Ming, called the Merciless. This part was taken by the venerable character actor Charles Middleton, who had made his reputation playing wicked landlords and corrupt bankers. Like Crabbe, he was perfect. Looking like a thin Mao Tse-tung, with silken mustaches drooping to his waist, Middleton was evil incarnate, surely one of the all-time great screen villains. Ming himself had, apparently, only two ambitions in life: to kill our hero and take over the world. To these ends, he fought like a hungry scorpion, inspiring us all with respect for his prowess and despisal for his methods. Still, we had a certain fondness for him and were always relieved when he managed, at the last instant, to escape Flash's wrath.

Flash Gordon's Trip to Mars, directed by Beebe and Robert F. Hill, was a fitting conclusion to the trilogy. This serial contained all the wondrous elements of the first two, plus a few of its own. From it, and from the others, we received visions, excitements and fears that would stay with us probably forever. Who could ever wholly forget such characters as Vulcan, the hawkman; noble Prince Barin; old Doctor Zarkov; the Clay People (who emerged from the walls of hidden caves); the Tree Men; or such things as the Bridge of Light (an electronic

beam which could support the weight of men); the Atomic
Elevator (which, instead of going through the laborious process
of transporting you from one floor to another, disassembled
your molecules and reassembled them, a split-second later, at
the desired location—and this thirty years before *The Fly!*);
the Ray Pistols (which shot stunning, paralyzing, or killing
high-frequency sound waves, depending upon the adjustment);
the musical score (largely from *Bride of Frankenstein*); the
great rocket ships which could fly from Mars to Earth but were
not even equipped with landing gear (they skidded to a stop);
or any of the thousand-and-one bright moments contained in
that magnum opus?

No, Katzman never matched the Flash Gordon trilogy, but
it was an improbable undertaking at best. For Flash, and Flash
alone, seemed able to combine wild science-fiction and fantasy
with plausible human situations. Unlike Buck Rogers (also
played by Crabbe), he was just enough larger than life to remain recognizable. He had faults. He was vulnerable. He was
a person.

Still, this is not to say we put down Sam's contributions.
Through his aegis, we were able to enjoy such Sunday friends
as Dick Tracy, Terry and the Pirates, Captain Midnight, Don
Winslow of the Navy, the Phantom, and most of the other
comic-strip adventurers. They were uniformly disappointing
at first encounter, but I think we understood the movie-makers'
problems and made allowances accordingly. These serials were
all popular, as were those based on such radio personalities as
Jack Armstrong, the All-American Boy; the Green Hornet;
King of the Royal Mounted; the Shadow; the Lone Ranger;
et al.

The Katzman quickie technique soon reduced the mechanics of serial production to an unbelievable degree. In the silent period, shooting an episode in ten days was considered normal. Woody Van Dyke, the noted director, was once paid a generous bonus for every chapter of an opus that he completed in a week's time. But *Jack Armstrong* and its kindred were put in the can at the incredible rate of an episode *every two days!* The thirty-one reels of a fifteen-chapter serial (three reels were allotted to the first chapter to allow for "character development") would be finished in thirty-one days of camera work.

The methods used to achieve this speed are interesting and indicative of the changes which have reduced the once mighty film industry to its present struggling position. In addition to cutting-in thousands of feet of "stock" footage, of scenery, distant action and assorted catastrophes, the producer generally specified that standing sets be used. Two units—director, camera crew and property men—worked simultaneously at top pace with the actors alternating between the sets. The hero and heroine might be attempting to escape from the menace on one stage while the heavies were pursuing them on another. By placing his villains in a central setting, say a laboratory or office, the writer could arrange for enough footage to be shot in this limited area to carry the threat throughout the entire film. Many a heavy has worked two days and appeared in all thirty-one reels.

"We never knew what the story was, really," says John Hart (who played the lead simultaneously in *The Phantom, Jack Armstrong* and *The Lone Ranger*). "All we did was memorize our lines as fast as we could and hurry from one unit to the other." In shooting *Jack Armstrong*, this rushing from set to set was brought to a climax of economy by filming a fight which took place in the back of a truck while the principals were being transported from studio to location. Taking advantage of every opportunity such as this was expected of a competent director.

The Hollywood legend about the serial director who suffered a fatal heart attack while on location but whose shooting was so well planned that production went on around his blanket-covered form, may or may not be factual, but it is indicative of the demands of this slam-bang calling. Although their fame scarcely reached outside the tight little community of the profession, the good cliff-hanger director was every bit as skilled as the giant names who drew assignments to do the Colossal and the Stupendous. Pacing the film action by their own exertions, these men also needed the practical abilities of a mechanical engineer coupled with a truly flamboyant imagination to bring in—at modest cost, remember—the hazards dreamed up by writers.

Spencer G. Bennett, whose intimate acquaintance with such effects stemmed from a vigorous career as a stunt man, was undoubtedly the master. A quick-thinking and ingenious director, as well as one who had a superb flair for comedy, Bennett is credited with often working the cast uphill out of a valley in a moving sequence to take advantage of the last rays of setting sun. Between 1925, when he took over from George B. Seitz, and 1956, when he put the last serial in the can, Bennett directed fifty-two of the hangers. These included most of the later gems about which we wax nostalgic, and such famous releases as the Tunney *Fighting Marine,* the original of

Edgar Wallace's *Green Archer, The Last Frontier* (starring Creighton Chaney, later Lon Chaney, Jr.) *Rogue of the Rio Grande* (one of Myrna Loy's first appearances) and *The Valley of Vanishing Men* with Bill Elliot and Slim Summerville, one of the best Western serials ever made.

Bennett was also the director of *The Mysterious Pilot,* which grabbed us all with its great stunt flying. Captain Frank Hawks, one of the world's finest speed-and-stunt pilots, was not allowed to do the aerobatics, Bennett relates, but was provided with a double for these scenes! "Too risky," ruled the studio heads; but Hawks, a hard man to keep on the ground, nearly finished the serial prematurely and came within an inch of killing himself while on a routine pleasure flight.

So facile was Bennett, and so succinct his directorial edicts, that he often made the camera setup for a scene and hurried away to place another waiting crew in position while the action was being filmed—never seeing the drama he was creating. He could move into such time-saving methods because he had, during his career as an actor and stunt man, survived most of the situations through which he now coached his actors.

W. S. Van Dyke, on the other hand, worked with a close friend and stunt man extraordinary, Bob Rose, who became an extension of his own ability to devise stringent hazards. Van Dyke directed many of the Ruth Roland adventures and when the going got absolutely too rough for the durable Ruth, Rose was called in from the bench.

Both Van Dyke and his sidekick were put to the test in a Roland serial when they concluded a chapter with Ruth escaping from a group of hungry cannibals.

Just as she was apparently safe, having eluded her pursuers, she found her path ending at the top of a sheer cliff with the sea raging below, at which point the head-hunters appeared in the distance brandishing their bows and spears.

Theatre patrons had a week to think about the means the heroine was going to use to save her fair skin, but Van Dyke had to begin shooting the following Monday.

Remembering a rock which stood out several hundred feet from the shore farther down the coast, Van Dyke had the rock turned into a tiny island, with a lookout (a hut atop a simulated palm tree) erected on it. Miss Roland was to spot the haven, breast the breakers and climb into the hut. The natives, apparently averse to water, rage on the cliff impotently —for a while. Then a lowbrowed Edison among the tribe begins shooting flaming arrows into the hut. Ruth, subbed for by Bob Rose, is trapped again. Unable to climb down the pole because of the fire, or to jump, because she could never clear the "island," it seems certain that she is in for cremation. And the cocky savages leave in pursuit of unroasted game.

The episode was supposed to end here, and the opening of the next chapter to begin with Ruth frantically rocking the pole so as to be thrown out into the sea. Van Dyke had rigged a wire to accomplish this effect but it broke on the first tug and Rose looked in a fair way to be cooked for real.

However, the desperate stunter did get the pole swaying and it finally parted with a loud crack, but fell in the wrong direction—*toward* the narrow, shallow channel and land.

Rose, skirts flying, made a determined leap to clear the island. In a fine serial finish, a huge wave broke at precisely the right instant, filling the channel with water to a safe depth and swallowing Rose in a welter of foam.

As the cameras had never stopped grinding, the sequence was printed and used for a truly tremendous conclusion.

Since doubles were employed on the later quickies for only the most hazardous stunts, during the Comic Strip era, acting ability was several notches down the list of requirements.

"Can you run? Can you swim? Can you fight? This is what we asked," says Sam Katzman. "If they could act, too, that was fine."

John Hart and others of his calling were selected in many instances because they could fall, handle horses, or ride like experts. A handsome face and the talent to manage more than two expressions were the extra qualities that insured the best jobs. Of course, there was no guarantee that the handsome features would remain intact. Fights, though staged by veteran stunt men, had to look real. "If the director wasn't satisfied with the way you pulled your punches, you would find yourself getting really killed," Hart recalls. In addition, the explosions, of which there were an inordinate number in *Jack Armstrong,* were as real as black powder could make them and the principles were just as near to the blast as they seemed to be when viewed from the comfort of a theatre seat.

The "plot" of *Jack Armstrong,* incidentally—and for purposes of comparison—concerned the threat of a group of evil citizens to destroy the world with a death-ray gun. Their scheme was simplicity itself: They would take the ray gun into orbit around the earth by means of a rocket ship which, presumably, the inventor of the ray gun had also perfected, and demand ransom. Jack, learning of the dastardly plot, undertook to thwart the action. The rocket was based on a desert island populated by a tribe of fire-worshiping savages who were loyal to the destroyers. And they *were* destroyers. Between being cast into fire pits, hurled to vicious wild animals, assaulted by knife throwers and blown up in various tricky ways, Jack, Billy and Betty, Uncle Jim and a luscious sarong-clad female member of the tribe whose name escapes all concerned, may be counted fortunate to have emerged with whole skins.

Of the writers from whose brains these remembered epics sprang, little is known, except that they were a breed apart. Not many Hollywood scriveners today could be counted on to turn out a script several times fatter than *Gone with the Wind*, rich in incident and bristling with action, in less than a week —yet that was what was expected of the serial creators. George Plympton was responsible for the screenplays of over one hundred serials, while Frank Leon Smith accounted for at least that many.

Serials are gone now, part of our past and part of our heritage. The last one, *Blazing the Overland Trail*, was made in 1956, and no more have followed. To the question, *Why?* there are hundreds of answers, and all of them are probably true. Industry people blame the ubiquitous glass-eyed monster, Television. Free serial-type entertainment on the small screens certainly did chop into theatre revenues in every bracket, but there's more to it than that. Television, for all its well-known mediocrity, did help raise the level of sophistication. Kids nowadays are exposed to news events in a manner undreamed of in our generation. Whereas we could glance at the war headlines or not, and often we did not, world developments are inescapable in the average TV-ridden living room. One of the results is a working knowledge of areas which were once presented to us as virgin territory—and whatever fiendish creatures the serial-men visualized could well populate those areas, for all we knew.

Today, Darkest Africa is a strife-torn group of emerging nations; Transylvania, ancestral home of unmentionable horrors, is part of a country which has fallen under Red domination; China is a gray land of Communes—and we'd better not call them fiends or they might blow us to hell.

Then, too, the kids today are having second thoughts about such matters as good and evil—matters that never concerned *us* at all. Jonas Salk is gradually replacing Flash Gordon as a hero, and that's probably to the good, for it demonstrates progress. But progress is like a burglar who robs you of a dear possession and leaves something more valuable in its place. You're pleased about the new gift, but you're sorry somehow that you couldn't have kept them both.

The kids today are smarter than we were, and I wish them well in their wisdom. But I wouldn't want to trade.

Who's got
the funnies?

IT IS fashionable, in our present intellectual climate, to denigrate, pooh-pooh and otherwise put down anything that has a purely visceral appeal. We are grown sophisticated—willing to chuckle but afraid to laugh. For when we laugh, we lose control: off guard and helpless, bellies aching, eyes full of tears, we step back a million years, naked and mole-blind, to join our forefathers in their caves. This, apparently, is a bad scene. It is not enough to be human any more. In this age of super-weapons and super-gadgets, we must be super-humans, and that means no weaknesses. Yet it is all a vast and silly deceit, and there is no greater proof of this than the fact that comic strips are still being enjoyed.

In older, simpler days, we were less leery of our emotions—possibly because we hadn't been tipped that they were signs of frailty. Everybody had his favorite comic strips then and was happy to say so, intellectuals not excepted. One of our Presidents, Franklin Delano Roosevelt, managed to get his mind off World War II by following the exploits of Chester Gould's axe-jawed hero, Dick Tracy. (Unable to endure the suspense of waiting until Monday for the solution to Friday's dilemma, F.D.R. would occasionally phone the strip's syndicate for a sneak preview.) At about the same time —when new Chevrolets were selling for $475, delivered, when short ribs cost seven and a half cents a pound, and Lucky Strike green was preparing to go to war—King George VI relaxed, during the blitz, with *The Little King,* Emperor Hirohito perused his smuggled copies of *Blondie* and A. Hitler giggled over the antics of *his* favorite, *Mickey Mouse.* Mussolini succeeded in banning all comics in Italy, but national protest forced him to exempt *Popeye.*

Then, in the midst of our laughter, some sourpuss came along and pointed out that comics were a lowbrow form of amusement, fit only for kids. Fortunately, the syndicates and newspaper editors didn't buy this. They continued to distribute and print comics, which they would not have done had they honestly felt that the appeal was solely to kids, for the purpose of comics has always been to sell newspapers, and it's Papa, not Junior, who buys these newspapers.

So it was that, as comics lost their respectability, they actually gained in popularity—no surprise to anyone who remembers what happened to liquor during Prohibition—and before long they were delighting millions who might otherwise never have been attracted.

With Walt Kelly's *Pogo* came such a wealth of lunacy and fun and wit and warmth that this irrepressible opossum and his Okefenokee friends soon made even the most jaded readers forget themselves. It was not, of course, the first time they had thus forgotten themselves. Earlier, there had been Crockett Johnson's whimsical *Barnaby* and before that Percy Crosby's talky, philosophical *Skippy*, around both of which formed smug in-groups, but with *Pogo* in-groupiness gave way to love —even among hardened cynics. When the cynics realized what they were doing, they explained that, of course, *Pogo* could hardly be considered a comic strip. Rubbish. Though better drawn than most, and better written, *Pogo* was indeed a comic strip, and in the classic tradition, at that. Kelly cliques sprang up all over the country. He became the darling of the intellectuals, hailed by them as a great comedic spirit, an incisive commentator on our mores—as everything except what he was, and is: a professional cartoonist. In time, Kelly became famous. He was In. But this did not impress him. He had been famous and In with the kids for years before the intelligentsia finally caught up.

With the arrival of *Peanuts,* the unofficial ban was lifted. It had to be. For breathed there a man with soul so dead that to himself he had not said, "Good grief!"? Could anyone in his right mind be expected to occupy the same world as Charles M. Schulz and not acknowledge the fact humbly and in gratitude? Charlie Brown, who was born between hydrogen-bomb tests, asked only one thing of us: that we love him. He needn't have bothered. Yet, just like *Pogo, Peanuts* was "merely" a comic strip; if anything, more traditional than most.

Inevitably the tide began to turn. Mature, intelligent people began to let it slip that they followed *Li'l Abner*. And of course *Steve Canyon* was always worth a look. Thumping good story values in that one. And, it went without saying, *Beetle Bailey*—well, after all, didn't President Eisenhower himself admit that this was a favorite of his? Didn't Grace Kelly's father express enthusiasm for *The Phantom?* And one couldn't really afford to ignore *Dick Tracy,* could one? And *King Aroo,* needless to say. And *Tarzan.* And . . .

At Boston University $37,000 will be spent in a study of the history and influence of comic strips. There are already several books on the subject. We are told it is all right for us to dig the funnies because they are of vast sociological and cultural significance. And already there are mutterings to the effect that they are art, of the highest order and deepest importance.

Maybe so. If, as the *Encyclopaedia Britannica* tells us, art is "anything which is not natural," then there is no reason to withhold the handle, particularly not if it will comfort us after we have split a gut over the funnies. But even if there's more to art than that, even then the comics might qualify; a few of them, anyway; the best of them. In terms of beauty, imagination, communication, emotional response, and general good to the world, whose creation is more deserving of the laurel—Salvador Dali's *The Invention of the Monsters* or *Peanuts?*

Before 1895, there was no such thing as a comic strip. The newspapers of the period were gray with tight, tiny rows of type, unrelieved except by an occasional realistic sketch or a laboriously detailed cartoon of the Hogarth school. A funny animal feature, *The Little Bears and Tigers,* began to appear regularly in the *San Francisco Examiner* in 1892 but it had no real continuity and is mentioned only because its creator, James Swinnerton, was later to become a major influence on comic artists. The first bona fide ancestor of our present family of comic-strip characters was a bizarre little elf called the Yellow Kid. He came into existence July 7, 1895, born of a happy union between Richard Felton Outcault and Joseph Pulitzer. In keeping with tradition, neither of these gentlemen had any inkling of what he was starting. Pulitzer, whose *New York World* was locked in mortal combat with William Randolph Hearst's *Journal,* simply wanted a gimmick to sell more newspapers. The gimmick, however, was not a trail-blazing excursion into comic art but, instead, the newly discovered color printing process. Pulitzer had it working fine, except for yellow. For some reason, no one could make this color dry properly. So Pulitzer decided to experiment—publicly. For the purpose, he called in staff-artist Outcault and laid the problem before him. Outcault responded with a variation on his popular Hogan's Alley drawings. Into the New York slum settings, replete with mobster brats, broken bums and scrofulous dogs, he inserted a wildly improbable creature belonging neither to Hogan's Alley nor to the natural world. It—no one could guess the gender—was about half the size of the smallest child, yet with its mandarin features, its bald head and conch-shell ears, it was clearly no child. (Years later Milton Caniff revived the Yellow Kid in *Terry and the Pirates,* changing his name to Connie, adding a few feet to his stature, but otherwise sticking to the original. Few but insiders ever got the joke.) Outcault himself never stated the reason for the *outré* features, but for the flowing nightgown there was full justification: it was a perfect proving ground for the color tests.

The Yellow Kid (from whose name the phrase "yellow journalism" is said to have been derived) became popular at the outset. So popular, in fact, that even after Pulitzer gave up wondering where the yellow went, the panel was continued. Soon thereafter, Hearst lured Outcault to the *Journal,* but Pulitzer retained legal rights to his feature and shortly there were two Yellow Kids—each a tremendous hit.

It is difficult to understand why. Despite his sagacious countenance, the Kid was a vicious little hoodlum, taking keen delight in such boyhood pranks as torturing Negroes, hectoring dog-catchers and breaking windows. The captions, talcumed throughout each drawing, were as phony as an operatic laugh, depending for their effect almost entirely upon dialect and freakish word combinations ("Gee Dis Beats De Carpet Which Is Hard To Beat"). Certain representatives of the "genteel readership" posted sharp protests, but to no avail. The Kid was a winner.

He stayed a winner for two years; then, when people began to tire of the back-alley humor, Outcault came up with *Buster Brown,* who differed from the Kid in that he was rich and of a somewhat less homicidal nature.

Still we have no comic strip as such, but we are getting close. In 1897 an elegantly mustachioed young artist moved East. His name was Rudolph Dirks. He possessed an uncertain line, an average imagination and a lucky star. The latter manifested itself when the *Journal's* comic editor, Rudolph Block, suggested that Dirks put together a feature based upon German humorist Wilhelm Busch's famous rapscallions, Max and Moritz. Dirks experimented with his adaptation, renamed the mischievous heroes the Katzenjammer Kids, and made the speech "balloon" an integral part of graphic humor in America.

"Mit dose kids society iss nix," commented one of dose kids' victims, and he was right. Hans and Fritz were rowdies, but unlike Outcault's grotesques, they perpetrated their maddening japes in a spirit of fun. By 1900 they had become a permanent landmark on the American cultural scene, beloved by millions.

As in the case of Outcault, Dirks was seduced away from his home paper, and out of this came a now famous legal dispute. The *Journal* claimed ownership of the Kids. So did Dirks. The courts decided in favor of both. Dirks could continue with his characters, but he could not retain the title. Result: the *Journal* hired H. H. Knerr to carry on *The Katzenjammer Kids,* while Dirks chose the title *The Captain and the Kids* and went on drawing and writing as before. There was never much to choose between the two. Dirks was zanier and had a better grip on the *Ach! Himmel!* dialog; Knerr drew with a surer line. Both creations were splendid.

Legend has it that Bud Fisher created the first honest-to-gosh comic strip (as we understand the term: four or five panels running across the page, either developing an episode or telling a complete story). The truth is that Clare Briggs beat everyone to the punch with his *A. Piker Clerk,* in 1904. The strip was not very good, however. But neither was Fisher's strip much to shout about until, on March 29, 1908, a magical accident occurred. Mr. Augustus Mutt, a flashily dressed racing tout, had been planned as a lone hero. Although no one could claim that he was a sensation, he had a certain appeal, and for the most part, people liked him. Then, one day, Fisher decided to give Mutt a friend. He would call the friend Jeff, after the fighter Jim Jeffries. Appropriately, the two met for the first time in an insane asylum, and the rest, as they say, is history.

Mutt and Jeff became the most popular comic creation in the world, and Harry Conway Fisher became the first cartoonist to earn $1000 a week. Now Fisher is dead, but, after fifty years, his characters are still going strong, carried on in the old tradition by Fisher's one-time assistant, Al Smith.

After *Mutt and Jeff,* the comics stopped being a novelty and became a respectable occupation. Of course there were no training schools then, and most of the artists came either from the sports departments (as Fisher did) or from magazines. For some reason, the magazine illustrators didn't cut the condiments, perhaps because they were too good. More often than not, their pictures were so well drawn that people forgot the stories. An exception, however, was Winsor McCay. Having established an enviable reputation in the book and magazine field, he moved into the comics, bringing with him an ability with pen and ink that has seldom been excelled to this day. He had the good sense not to try for funny animals or humorous grotesques. Instead, he created the first of the "realistic strips," *Little Nemo.* The draftsmanship, with its unprecedented use of perspective, and its Maxfield Parrish–like settings, was a miracle of skill combined with imagination. The story itself was fantastic, following a typical seven- or eight-year-old boy through the land of his dreams. No one with eyes in his head could resist the strip. And it is a mark of the ageless beauty of *Little Nemo* that when it was reprinted, forty years after its first appearance, most people thought it was a new feature.

According to Arthur Brisbane, Harry Hershfield's *Abie the Agent* was "the first of the adult comics in America." Hershfield produced a gentle strip about a mild, sweet-tempered Jew and charmed the world, for a while. Abie spoke in an odd dialect, when he spoke at all, which was seldom, and probably accomplished much in the fight against prejudice.

August 3, 1913, saw the first appearance of *Bringing Up Father* and its protagonist, the mighty Jiggs. To George McManus, who had already achieved fame with such pioneering efforts as *Alma and Oliver, Snoozer, Let George Do It* and *Panhandle Pete,* it was only another comic strip. But Jiggs caught on fast. People fell in love with the little Irishman and sympathized with him in his problem, which was that of a simple, honest man who likes the simple, honest things of life (viz., corned beef and cabbage, billiards, poker) but is forbidden to enjoy them. Jiggs and his termagant wife Maggie were *nouveaux riches.* After many years of happy penury, suddenly they had become millionaires. Jiggs did not see why this should make any great difference in his life, but Maggie had other ideas. Now that we're rich, she said, brandishing her rolling pin, we're going to act the part. Whereupon Jiggs found himself a prisoner of his own ambition, forced to brave the wrath of wife, daughter, servants and business associates, in order to partake of pleasures he'd previously taken for granted. The message was comforting, particularly during the depression: don't hanker after material wealth—you might end up like Jiggs.

Of course, you might also end up like that other son of Eire, George McManus, who lived a rich, full life, apparently undisturbed by the fat bank account he acquired thanks to Jiggs—whom he strikingly resembled, by the way.

Not so well remembered as Jiggs, but equally famous in his day, was *Barney Google.* Barney began life, in 1919, as a bug-eyed shrimp devoted, like Augustus Mutt, to the Sport of Kings. He made bets, lost them, and cringed at the invective of a shrewish and domineering wife, and it appeared that he would go the way of a hundred similar clichés. Then, on July 17, 1922, Barney met Sparkplug. No sadder horse existed, no heart was so easily broken nor so full of love for Google. The little fellow's character changed almost overnight. Now that someone really cared for him, he dropped his wiseacre mannerisms and became, in time, the sweet soul Sparkplug had known him to be all along.

Barney rode high for almost two decades; then his creator, Billy DeBeck, introduced him to the various members of an Ozark family named Smith, and that was the beginning of Barney's decline. No saint has ever been able to match a rascal in popularity. And no more rascally figure than Snuffy Smith could be found on the comic scene. Snuffy, his long-suffering wife Lowizie, and his wild nephew Jughaid, thrust Barney from the center of the stage and, with an angry "Balls o'fire!" took over the strip. Together, these children of DeBeck's imagination contributed more valuable words and phrases to the public vocabulary than any group of real-life people had done for twenty years. From them we inherited "google-eyed," "heebie-jeebies," "tetched in the haid," the aforementioned "Balls o'fire!" and many more. DeBeck died in 1942, but there was no change in Barney or Snuffy. Fred Lasswell wisely refused to "bring them up to date."

Another example of a minor character's taking over from the ostensibly more important characters may be found in Raeburn Van Buren's strip, which for some reason is still called *Abbie 'n' Slats,* although an unsanitary old curmudgeon known as Bathless Groggins long ago took the stage away from the title twosome. Van Buren, an able draftsman, usually finds some excuse to involve Bathless in adventures with dusky harem beauties. They are decorously brassièred, as a rule, but once Van Buren managed to slip past editors a harem episode in which one or two of the houris were drawn bare-bosomed, complete with nipples. Sad to relate, the bras were back on in the very next episode.

Now the question of art must raise its Janus head again, for it is time to speak of *Krazy Kat*. George Herriman was an artist in the sense that he drew pictures; he was a great artist in the sense that the pictures he drew were examples of great comic art; whether or not he was an artist in the sense of our current interpretation of that ill-used word is a matter of personal opinion. Learned students of the field have ranked him with Chaplin, and his creation, Krazy, with Don Quixote. Others think he was simply a good cartoonist who happened to have a screw or two loose in his head. Out of the debate one fact emerges healthy and unbruised: Herriman and Krazy were the most original fun-makers of their time. They were natural phenomena, without ancestors and without heirs, absolutely unique in a world where nothing new is supposed to happen under the sun. There was nothing like them before. There has been nothing like them since. And that cannot be said of any other comic strip. Who can forget those mysterious, ever-changing landscapes (located somewhere in mythical Coconico County); that trinity of fools—Offissa Pup, Ignatz Mouse and Krazy—who existed for and by themselves; the inevitable brick (POW!) hurled with love; and the jail that appeared like magic out of the Coconico dust? From the chaos came order, and no one questioned the order, for like the genius he was—if only at so humble a profession as cartooning—Herriman managed to create a microcosm and make it work.

A lesser talent was that of Sidney Smith. Nevertheless, because of a shrewd bargaining sense and the popularity of *The Gumps,* Smith became the first millionaire in the business. Unfortunately, he never got to enjoy his wealth, for on the day he signed his now-famous million-dollar contract he was involved in an automobile accident, suffering fatal injuries. The Gumps weren't particularly funny, nor were they well drawn. Andy, the protagonist, managed to look like a circus freak—huge nose, cigar-shaped mustache, no chin, a grotesque hole in his neck for a mouth—and, at the same time, like everybody's dad: a peculiar triumph. Min, his wife, was simply a witch. Yet they were accepted by America, and soon the Family Situation dominated the comics. Most of these strips were poor, but they prepared the way for such genuinely worthwhile efforts as *Out Our Way, The Timid Soul* and *Blondie.*

Neither *Toonerville Trolley* nor *Harold Teen* was a family situation strip, though both were about families. Fontaine Fox gave us a stylized, economical, frequently sophisticated and always zany feature: the trolley began as his memory of an actual conveyance, but it is difficult to believe that Fox ever knew anyone remotely like The Terrible Tempered Mister Bang or Powerful Katrinka or Mickey (Himself) McGuire. Carl Ed's *Harold Teen* started at the top and stayed there for generations. Harold and his friend Shadow always managed to keep a jump ahead of the real-life teen-agers, and so the characters never became dated.

In an odd way, *Smokey Stover* was born dated. Yet Bill

Holman's wacky fireman never has conformed to an actual period, perhaps because he has never lived in an actual world. Understand NOTARY SOJAC and FOO and you understand the strip.

By the time of World War I, the technique of the comic strip had reached its present form. There have been refinements since then, but no significant changes. The across-the-page panels, the "speech balloons," the heavy outlines, the sound effects, even the punctuation (sentences are never said in comicland; since the days when periods, being tiny, got lost in the crude printing processes, characters have always exclaimed!!!!) —all were standard operating procedure forty-five years ago. For some reason, people picked up instantly on the cartoonists' various codes and symbols, even while they were vociferously rejecting the less arcane experiments of modern artists, poets and composers. If a cartoonist wished to get across the idea that his character was in the grip of anxiety or fear, he drew little droplets of perspiration about the character's head. Embarrassment was shown by a number of lines across the face, surprise by a general paralysis of the body, a bugging of the eyes and a straight-up flight of hat and hair. No emotion, however subtle, escaped the swift invention of those early comic artists. They were able, through a thousand and one stylized devices, to depict the whole complex structure of man's nature. Stream of consciousness, for example, was a commonplace in comics before most of us had heard of James Joyce. Surrealism and Dadaism outraged a world which had long before accepted the fanciful flights of George Herriman. Even before the turn of the century, comic artists were making use of sound effects, too. At first they all relied upon the stock BANG! POW! and SOCK! then Dirks began to think up new words and the others followed suit. Soon each cartoonist had his own store of effects, some ideal, some outlandish. In fifty years, for example, guns have gone: BANG! BLAM! CRASH! CRACK! CHOW! and even BURP! (At Dell, publishers of the world's largest line of comic magazines, there is a rule which forbids the depiction or mention of alcohol, or any establishment brewing, selling, or dispensing it. A puckish cartoonist finally satisfied a lifetime ambition by making his gun go: BAR-ROOM!)

For a long time, the comics were meant to be comical. Frank King started *Gasoline Alley* (in 1919) as a humorous comment on America's love affair with automobiles, for example, but the strip soon changed into a Family Situation and humor was traded for warmth. Walt Wallet and his foundling son Skeezix exuded appeal, behaving in a manner which most people took to be normal. Nothing startling here, nothing wild —except the wildest and most startling innovation of all, begun by King. These comic characters, and these alone, obeyed the laws of time. While Mutt and Jeff and Skippy and Harold Teen remained the same age always, existing in one suspended moment of forever, the Wallet family grew older every day, just like people; we watched Skeezix turn into an adult, before our eyes.

Harold Gray's *Little Orphan Annie* was also realistic, but Gray's methods were different. Annie is over thirty-five years old now, but apart from a slightly more attractive hair-do, she is still the same spavined, piteous, blank-eyed little waif the world first took to its heart in 1924. (Those famed blank eyes sprouted pupils, suddenly, for a short period in the forties, but the heresy was soon squelched.) The strip has always been straight soap opera. Annie and her overage dog, Sandy, have blundered in and out of situations that would tax the resources of Superman, but invariably Annie has emerged daisy-fresh and undismayed. The truth is, she is far from piteous. Thanks to her creator, she is perhaps the most willful and stubborn female since Carrie Nation, and probably more dangerous. In a strip that reaches millions of young readers, Annie has advocated capital punishment, abolition of unions, impeachment of a President (F.D.R.) and the establishment of an aristocratic government—preferably headed by a munitions magnate along the lines of the story's beneficent hero, Daddy Warbucks.

Science-fiction would seem a natural theme for comics, but only three such strips managed to take hold. *Buck Rogers* was the first. Created by John F. Dille in 1929, and drawn by Lieutenant Dick Calkins, this strip—set five hundred years in the future—became an immediate hit with the public. The ideas were far-out—space travel, paralysis ray pistols (remember *zap?*) and—in a 1939 panel—the devastation of an atomic war, after which we were urged to join the Buck Rogers Solar Scouts so that Earth might be defended against such attack. Buck's cohorts were a shapely blonde female soldier named Lieutenant Wilma Deering and a bulk-headed scientific genius, Doctor ("Heh!") Huer. Buck's antagonists were snarling, mustachioed Killer Kane, the sinuous Ardala, and assorted extra-terrestrials such as the Tiger Men of Mars. *Flash Gordon,* which came after *Buck,* took place not in the future but on the fictional planet Mongo, ruled by the strangely Asian emperor, Ming the Merciless. Flash was an athletic Apollo of an Earthman, and, like Buck Rogers, numbered among his cronies a beautiful chick (Dale Arden) and a Great Scientist (black-bearded Dr. Zarkov). Thanks to Alex Raymond's superb draftsmanship, the most outlandish other-worldly creatures (hawkmen, lionmen, two-headed dragons) were lifelike, hence frightening. Also life-like, but far from frightening, were Alex Raymond's females—Princess Aura, the Witch Queen of Mongo, and Dale herself —most of whom in the strip's heyday went around in get-ups that were translucent, or low-cut, or slit-skirt, or belly-baring, or all four. *Brick Bradford* used a time-traveling machine (the Time Top) as his gimmick. It was effective and allowed Brick —a Flash-like hero with curly locks and a way with curvilinear, underdressed females—to engage in many wild adventures in time and space; but the strip was not distinctive enough to command a great following, and so, after a few years, Brick Bradford rode his Time Top into the past, where he remains.

Alley Oop began in the past, but this vaguely Popeye-shaped caveman soon established a record for restlessness un-matched by any other comic character. When his creator, V. T. Hamlin, tired of the distant Fictitious Era (zillions of years ago, when men rode pet dinosaurs), he catapulted Oop through time to the twentieth century. For fifteen years the gruff, no-nonsense prehistoric man has been shuttling in and out of most of the great periods of history.

Perhaps neither fantasy nor science-fiction—in light of to-day's discoveries in the field of hypnosis—*Mandrake the Magi-cian* continues, after more than two decades, to enchant Ameri-cans. With his tiny mustache, patent-leather hair, top hat and opera cape, Mandrake looks either like an old-time movie heavy or the guy who never found out that not all hair dressings are greasy. He is neither. He is the world's greatest hypnotist, numbering among his accomplishments the power to create individual and mass hallucinations at a moment's notice and to turn his head into a kind of motion-picture projector (he faces a blank wall, twin beams of light stab out from his eyes, and we are treated to a Technicolor movie of his inmost thoughts). Needless to say, Mandrake wages unending war with the underworld.

Prince Valiant must be included in this general category, for despite artist Hal Foster's meticulous attention to historical detail, he is essentially a fantasy man. The strip is alive with legends and myths, and always has been. It shows us what a Viking ship looks like but it also shows us a sword that sings and a dark sorcerer named Merlin who can pluck daemons out of the air and put them to work for him. Because of these threads of fantasy interwoven into the bright tapestry of fact, and because of Foster's magnificent artwork, the Duke of Windsor has stated, unequivocally, that *Prince Valiant* is "the greatest contribution to English literature in the past hundred years."

Chic Young's *Blondie* was perhaps the first strip to appeal equally to young and old. In the beginning she was an inane little flapper, and Dagwood was a John Held, Jr., type: rich, spoiled, stupid. All that changed when Dagwood's father disinherited him. He moved to the suburbs, went to work for Mr. Dithers, and settled in as an authentic piece of Americana. In him every housewife saw her bumbling but basically lovable husband; and in Blondie, every male saw the perfect wife.

A national favorite, after thirty years, is *Popeye.* He first appeared in a daily panel called *Thimble Theatre,* created by a fair-to-middling cartoonist named Elzie Segar. Segar had been drawing for several years, without any particular distinction. People sort of went for Olive Oyl and her addlepated brother Castor, but the feature could hardly have been termed a major success. Then came the one-eyed old spinach-eating sailor, and Segar soared to the heights of public acclaim. His drawing improved. It took on a weird, almost mystical quality. And so did his writing. In those days, *Popeye* was a fantasy, and the strip was filled with wild and wonderful creatures—Alice the Goon, with her body growth of fur; Eugene the Jeep, who could survive only if fed a daily ration of orchids; the infamous Sea Hag; and no less wild and no less wonderful, J. Wellington ("I'll gladly pay you tomorrow for a hamburger today") Wimpy—who single-handedly made the hamburger America's number one dish. Segar's contributions to the language were innumerable. In addition to *jeep* and *goon,* he gave us *Blow me down!* and *I yam what I yam an' tha's all I yam!* —surely one of the clearest statements of personal philosophy ever uttered. *Popeye* was continued after Segar's death, but not even the combined talent of Tom Sims and Bela Zaboly could duplicate the master's vision. Some fans still wish that the syndicate had decided to bury the creation with the creator, as was done in the case of *Krazy Kat.* (A memorial statue of the old sailor stands today in Crystal City, Texas.) For *Popeye* is exclusively a kid's strip now, cute as a bunny and dull as virtue.

No such description could ever apply to *Li'l Abner.* For twenty-five years this handsome, hulking hillbilly has been characterized as the Great American Boob, but Abner isn't a boob and neither is his author, Al Capp. Both are men of native, almost sinister intelligence, and though it is true that they make people laugh, it is also true that this laughter is more often bitter than joyful. Capp's subjects have always been serious. At one time or another he has dealt with almost every major issue of our era. But, like Swift, he is a profound pessimist, having faith only in man's sublime and transcendental stupidity. There is no stopping this stupidity, Capp seems to be saying, and there is no ignoring it. Therefore one must laugh.

In the strict sense, Capp is not a humorist at all, but a harlequin, singing funny songs in the court of a corrupt king. Charles Chaplin has said, "For me personally, Al Capp, with his delightful characters, opens new vistas of broad buffoonery with inspirational satire." John Steinbeck goes a step further: "I think Capp may very possibly be the best writer in the world today. I am sure that he is the best satirist since Laurence Sterne."

Despite his pessimism, his savage satire, and his coterie status, Al Capp has produced the most consistently amusing comic strip of them all. It may be that we enjoy laughing at ourselves, or it may simply be that we like the sugar coating so well that we don't mind the pill. It is certainly tasty sugar, compounded of great and distinctive drawing, succulent maidens, mad grotesques, unbridled imagination, and an argot so compelling that it has passed into the (ugh!) public vocabulary.

An additional secret to *Li'l Abner's* success is Capp's ability to keep in step with the times. His eyes and ears are open constantly, and they miss nothing. The same is true of Milton Caniff. He slipped into the comic world slightly ahead of Capp with a strip called *Dickie Dare*. It was not terribly inventive, but it was superbly rendered and carefully researched, and because of these qualities gained prestige. Caniff tired of Dickie after a while and thought up something new. It was roughly the same sort of thing, only with greater scope. He called it *Terry and the Pirates.*

For almost twenty years Caniff stuck with *Terry,* refining and improving the strip to perfection. Then he turned it over to George Wunder, who could copy his style but not duplicate it, and Caniff went on to even greater fame with his current creation, *Steve Canyon.* A cartoonist can work all his life and count himself fortunate if he manages one real success. Caniff has managed three. If he eventually tires of Canyon, the figure might very well become four.

We're in a slack period now. There haven't been many grand creations in the field, although we can point—with considerable pride—to *Pogo* and *Peanuts.* As such things are reckoned, those two are destined for immortality. And, who knows? Perhaps they indicate the end of a cycle and a return to the time when comics were all fun and warmth and love and mysteriousness, when we laughed without wondering why, and thrilled and shuddered, and were generally glad to be around.

O (sob) happy day!

The bloody pulps

THERE WAS a ritual.

It was dark and mysterious, as rituals ought to be, and—for those who enacted it—a holy and enchanted thing.

If you were a pre-pubescent American male in the twenties, the thirties, or the forties, chances are you performed the ritual. If you were a little too tall, a little too short, a little too fat, skinny, pimply, an only child, painfully shy, awkward, scared of girls, terrified of bullies, poor at your school work (not because you weren't bright but because you wouldn't apply yourself), uncomfortable in large crowds, given to brooding, and totally and overwhelmingly convinced of your personal inadequacy to any situation, then you certainly did. Because this ritual, unlike those of many orthodox religions, was a genuinely spiritual experience—if by this is meant, as the theologists would have us believe, an experience relating not to the corporeal but to the incorporeal self. It involved that human essence which transcends body and mind. It involved the *person*.

116

Generally, it took place in America. Specifically: under the covers, late at night, with the rest of the family off to their beds and you feeling safe, at last, in flicking up the switch on your battered brass Eveready flashlight; or in a dilapidated lean-to behind the garage, with the summer sun thrusting hot fingers through the cracks of warped and knotty sawdust-smelling boards; or atop the rickety, perilous platform of a tree house to the susurrus of bees working juices out of over-ripe plums; or in dank basements, or in cerement-scented attics; or in tin-can-and-broken-bottle strewn lots; or in the golden rushing silence of river banks. Whatever the location, the rites—not recognized as such by the uninitiated, but called, plainly, reading—were the same.

Step One: The joyful but cautious removal of the treasure from its place of concealment;

Step Two: The glancing in all directions for aunts, uncles, parents and other intruders;

Step Three: The assuming of a comfortable position;

Step Four: The perusal of the treasure's cover, a procedure involving ten seconds to ten minutes depending upon the cover's design;

Step Five: The placing of the treasure next to the nose and the heady inhalation of its unique miasma of dust, raw ink, wood pulp, age and glory;

Step Six: The apocalyptic devouring, by the spirit, through the mind and the eyes, of the treasure; the disengagement of the self from the body, from time and from space; finally the wild and dizzy soaring off to secret unmapped regions, places of stalwart heroes, insidious villains and girls upon whom one could always depend to expose at least one breast.

What were the objects of this not accidentally sensual-sounding ritual, the treasures thus enshrined?

The Pulps.

What were they?

Cheaply printed, luridly illustrated, sensationally written magazines of fiction aimed at the lower- and lower-middle-class American male.

Were they any good?

No. They were great.

Doc Savage, The Shadow, The Spider, G-8 and His Battle Aces, The Phantom, Adventure, Argosy, Blue Book, Black Mask, Thrilling Wonder Stories, Marvel Tales—and all the hundred-and-one other titles that bedizened the newsstands of America in the halcyon days—provided ecstasy and euphoria of a type unknown to this gloomy generation. They made to crawl deliciously young scalps now mostly bald. They inspired, excited, captivated, hypnotized—and, unexpectedly, instructed —the reckless young who have become the responsible middle-aged. Of course, they were infra dig. In line with the imperishable American concept that anything which is purely enjoyable must be a sin, the pulps were considered sinful. Although they were, at their worst (or best), fractionally as "objectionable" as the immoral, amoral, violent, perverted product available nowadays to any tennis-shoe-shod sub-teen who has the price of admission to a movie theatre or access to a television set, they were proscribed by most parents and all educators. Thus we indulged in them in much the same way that we indulged in the other purely enjoyable facts of life. Which was an altogether agreeable state of affairs. Although we weren't aware of it at the time, the disapproval and prohibition actually increased our pleasure, adding a welcome pinch of lawlessness to the experience. Fortunately, the psychologists of the day did not understand the special sweetness of the stolen watermelon. So they denounced the pulps, wrote tracts on the fearful consequences certain to befall those whose minds were polluted by "the newsstand trash" and otherwise did their best to create a nation of addicts.

Addicts we certainly were. We gave ourselves over wholly to the habit and pursuit of the most potent literary drug known to boy, and all of us suffer withdrawal symptoms to this day. No one ever kicked the pulps cold turkey. They were too powerful an influence. Instead, most of us tried to ease off. Having dreamed of owning complete sets, in mint condition, of all the pulp titles ever published, and having realized perhaps a tenth part of the dream—say, fifteen hundred magazines, or a bedroomful—we suffered that vague disenchantment which is the first sign of approaching maturity (sixteen, going on seventeen, was usually when it happened) and decided to be sensible. Accordingly, we stopped buying *all* the new mags as fast as they could appear, and concentrated instead upon a few indispensable items. Gradually we cut down until we were keeping up the files on only three or four, or possibly five or six, publications. After a few years, when we had left high school and taken unto ourselves wives and families, we got the number down to two. Which is where most of us stand today. We don't read the magazines, of course. But we go on buying them. Not regularly, and not in any sense because we want to, but because we must. It is an obligation, a duty, to the bright untroubled selves we were. To plunge any further into adulthood would be an act of betrayal.

But the times have betrayed us, anyway. The pulps, as we knew and loved them, are gone. The gaudy, gory covers, the dramatic interior illustrations, the machine-gun prose, the rough, rich-smelling, wood-chip-speckled paper—all gone. The so-called pulps of 1961 are nothing of the kind. They are slickly printed, slickly written echoes of their own great past. Look at *Argosy* now, and then think of the magazine as it was when H. Bedford Jones and A. Hyatt Verrill and Arthur Leo Zagat were waging their bloody Mongol wars; pick up the diminutive, pocket-size, light-weight *Amazing Stories* and try to imagine it twenty years ago when it was the size of a dictionary (unabridged) and more exciting than a ride in a roller coaster. Buy one of these emasculated ghosts and display it on a subway. Wait for the frowns, and go on waiting forever— there won't be any. The pulps are now socially acceptable, and I can think of no greater damnation of them.

Only the well-remembered "8-pagers" (*Toots and Caspar, Dick Tracy, Popeye the Sailor,* etc.) carried a greater stigma than the old-time adventure magazines.

Happily, no sober, critical evaluation of them is possible. Like any other narcotic, they defy rational analysis. One can speak of their effect, even of their ingredients, but not, without wearisome and unconvincing pomposity, of their causes. Something in them froze the addict's critical faculties. He might entertain a difference of opinion on the relative merits of Putnam's and Shelton's translation of *Don Quixote,* but on the subject of *Weird Tales* he was, and is, adamant.

Reacting with typically honest fury to criticism of one of his favorite pulp writers, the eminent regional novelist and historian August Derleth wrote not too long ago:

With that sublime, egocentric stupidity which characterizes a certain subspecies of frustrate which goes in for book-reviewing in order to find some compensation for its own singular lack of creative ability by deprecating the work of those who are creative, a reviewer recently brushed aside a book of supernatural tales as being, after all, "only pulp-fiction." The reviewer offered no evidence of being able to say just what stigma attached to writing for the so-called "pulp" magazines. There has, of course, always been this kind of pusillanimous condescension on the part of various small-souled and incredibly mentally-limited gentry who presume to set themselves up as "critics," but who never grow away from the status of pathetic hacks ekeing out a crepuscular existence in the meanest of all "writing" trades—that of chopping and carping away at the work of writers who have too much personal dignity to descend to the parasitic status of such frustrated hangers-on. . . .

Derleth is known to be a kindly and gentle man, but when it comes to the pulps—on which he, like so many otherwise rational beings, was brought up—he is as blind, deaf and dumb, and hypersensitive to criticism, as a boy in love. The girl may not be popular, or even respectable, but he loves her still and woe to those who take the affair lightly.

Of course the reviewer who enraged Derleth could not have been an addict, so he ought to be forgiven; particularly in that, no matter what he said, he was probably right. To the hooked, those wild and wonderful stories were all great; to the unhooked (a state of being that is difficult for the hooked to imagine), they were no doubt dreadful, hardly to be classed as literature.

It is true that they were unlike any other literature to which we had been exposed. Before our encounters with "Gripping,

Smashing Detective Stories" (as the editor of *Black Mask* described the contents of his magazine) and similar periodicals, we tended to think of adventures as belonging to a previous age. Buccaneers, Indians, Frontier Fighters, Soldiers of Fortune —all were in the past, we thought. Then we read the pulps and learned that adventure surrounded us, that danger was omnipresent, evil a threat to be countered at all odds, and science not a laboratory curiosity but, rather, an active tool. We learned a lot of other things, too, including the quaint but useful lesson that it is more rewarding to be a good guy than a bad guy.

Take Doc Savage (as we did, in large uncut doses). Here truly was a worthwhile idol, a man among men. The newspapers called him The Mental Marvel, The Scientific Genius, The Muscular Midas. His enemies called him "The Yankee Menace." He fought on the side of Right, inspiring fear and respect in those who would threaten the U. S. of A., instantaneous passion in all women who ever caught a glimpse of him, and joy in the hearts of his many fans. We loved him. For his indefatigable attacks on the fortress of Evil, surely; and for his incredible feats of derring do; but mostly we loved him because of his willingness to share with us the secrets of his self-development exercises. Doc was a model of fitness. The wisdom of the old fox shone from his "strange, flake-gold eyes," but his bronzed body was that of a young god: lithe, sinewy, powerful. Nor was this a happy accident of nature, but, rather, the result of rigid discipline. The Doc Savage Plan of Living was eventually made available to the general readership, "in answer to innumerable requests." However, the Editor warned us that: "Important as these exercises may be, and as much as they may accomplish in building you up physically, mentally and mor-

ally, they should be only the basis for bigger things in life."
What bigger things the Editor had in mind, we did not know.
If through the Plan of Living we attained the abilities of Doc
Savage (and the implication was that we would), then we must
be equal to anything, for the Man of Bronze was even more
accomplished than any of his five assistants—and *they* were the
best in the world:

BRIGADIER GENERAL THEODORE MARLEY BROOKS, "Ham" for
short, Harvard Law School's most distinguished graduate and
America's best-dressed man, who carried a natty black cane
within which nestled a slender sword tipped with a mysterious
sleep-inducing drug developed by

LIEUTENANT COLONEL ANDREW BLODGETT "MONK" MAYFAIR,
one of the world's greatest chemists, a shy, gentle, squeaky-
voiced man with the build of a gorilla and the tenacity of a
scorpion;

COLONEL JOHN RENWICK, engineer extraordinary, whose
gallon-pail fists came in handy whenever a thick door-panel
needed smashing in;

MAJOR THOMAS J. "LONG TOM" ROBERTS, an electrical wiz-
ard, sturdy of mind, frail of physique;

And, far from least, the archeologist and geologist, WILLIAM
HARPER LITTLEJOHN, whose specialty was the English language.
He would have sent us all scurrying to our dictionaries had not
author Kenneth Robeson thoughtfully translated his transcendental philological peregrinations. (As it was, "Johnny" did
contribute importantly to our vocabularies. For a time we all
used his colorful substitute for profanity: "I'll be superamalga-
mated!")

With this fabulous confederacy of adventurers, headed always by Clark Savage, Jr., M.D. (specializing in brain surgery when he was not fighting the international cartels of evil), we traveled under the earth's surface, beneath the sea, into palaces of ice at the North Pole, through the jungles of Southeast Asia, into vast caverns on the equator, and down the reeky slums of the world's biggest and most mysterious cities. We were introduced by Robeson (a nom de plume for pulpster Lester Dent) to Kant and Lombroso. We were imbued with a healthy respect for scientists in particular and education in general. How else, save through education, could Doc have invented such marvels as his machine pistol, which fired "mercy bullets," gas pellets or explosive shells at so fantastic a rate of speed that it sounded like the lowest note of a bull fiddle; or his capacity detector, which, like an old regenerative radio, emitted a squeal whenever its field was interrupted; or the candy bar that kept you awake and supplied vitamins at the same time; or the wrist radios, the automatic door openers, the self-contained underwater breathing apparatus, etc.?

Within two or three issues after its introduction, the *Doc Savage* magazine was selling 200,000 copies per month. Robeson/Dent cranked out over a hundred novel-length adventures, turning his Man of Bronze into the most popular fictional character of the period.

Then came the *Shadow*. He didn't exactly eclipse Doc, but he cast a hell of a dark pall over our hero. We thought it was because he was more believable. After all, didn't each story begin with the declaimer that it was "from the private annals of the Shadow, as told to Maxwell Grant"? Of course. It was no problem to believe that Lamont Cranston existed and that

the man known as the Shadow assumed his identity whenever
it was necessary for him to emerge from the blackness of the
city night to accomplish some high-level mission. Unlike Doc,
who operated in a realm where law-enforcement officers were
seldom present, Cranston carried on a regular fox-and-hounds
with the police, and in particular with Inspector Cardona. The
milieu, if not the situations, was recognizable.

Fans who knew this master crime-fighter only through his
radio adventures knew him not at all. For the real low-down,
you had to go to the magazines. There, in the pulpy pages, he
existed in all his weird and inexplicable glory.

From his sanctum in an unidentified warehouse (lit only
by a blue lamp), the Shadow communicated, through his contact man, Burbank, with a small army of operatives: Hawkeye,
a small-time crook; Cliff Marsland, a free-lance mobster; Harry
Vincent, sometime reporter; and the indispensable hackie, Moe
Shrevnitz. Upon receiving news of impending, or recently com-
mitted, crime, the Shadow would blend into the dimness of the
evening and appear—with or without his confederates—to challenge the worst of evils. A master of disguises, he did not rely
entirely on concealment: a bit of wax in the cheeks, a touch
of make-up here and there, an affected slouch, limp or drooped
shoulder, and he might become a bowery bum, a cripple or even
a scrubwoman. He was also a master psychologist, and in Maxwell Grant's straightforward prose (which was the actual cause
of the Shadow's ascendancy over Doc Savage) we read:

There Badger saw The Shadow.

The mysterious avenger had arrived close behind his quarry.
Silent in the doorway, he had observed every action that the crook

had made. For some strange reason, The Shadow stood weaponless. One gloved hand rested on the doorknob; the other was against the side of the doorway.

Coincidentally, Badger, in turning, had aimed his revolver directly toward the door. Had he faced an armed policeman, the mobster would have fired. But sight of The Shadow overwhelmed him. Blazing eyes made the wounded crook falter. His gun hand wavered; sagged.

A product of the underworld, Badger was one who had bragged often that he would like the chance to gain a pot shot at The Shadow. But in this crisis, Badger failed.

The Shadow had expected it.

To those of us who lived with the Shadow through two-score pulp-paper perils, the radio episodes were a considerable letdown. Aside from the bloodcurdling laugh and the sibilant assurance (delivered by Orson Welles) that "The Shadow knows what evil lurks in the hearts of men," we felt that there was too little resemblance between the radio show and the "real" adventures. The half-hour dramatizations were interesting enough, but really, the Shadow did not have to depend upon hypnosis (". . . the power to cloud men's minds") in order to make his way unseen across rooftops and through dim hallways. And, there was entirely too much hanky-panky with Margo Lane, a sex-interest who drifted into the magazine's previously chaste pages and did much to confirm our suspicion that women ought to leave important matters to men.

The scripts for the radio dramas were written by Harry Charlot, who died in a poisoning mystery as intriguing as any Shadow novel; but each of the 178 book-lengthers—7,500,000 words of print—was turned out by Maxwell Grant. How could it be otherwise? The very first story, called *The Living Shadow,* was introduced in this fashion:

> This is to certify that I have made a careful examination of the manuscript known as "The Living Shadow," as set down by Mr. Maxwell Grant, my raconteur, and do find it a true account of my activities upon that occasion. I have therefore arranged that Mr. Grant shall have exclusive privilege to such further of my exploits as may be considered of interest to the American public. Signed, The Shadow.

The Shadow Club, sponsored by the magazine's astute publishers, Street & Smith, soon had more than 50,000 enrolled. The invitation extended to prospective members was couched in the form of a moral obligation: "If you are interested in observing the law and doing all you can to make others observe it, then it is your duty to join The Shadow Club." Membership was free, but if you wished to wear the emblem of the club (in nickel-silver) you were obliged to enclose ten cents, in coin or stamps, to help defray part of the cost of manufacture and mailing. Like the Doc Savage Club emblem (in bronze, of course) this was a difficult bargain to resist, so most of us eventually signed the pledge: *I promise to bend all my efforts to give my moral, and, when called upon, actual support to uphold law and order and down crooks.*

Looking back on those two great heroes, Doc and the Shadow, one wonders what ever prompted the disapproving attitude held by adults. Search as they might through the corpus of English literature, they could not have found two such spotless, virtuous, moral and right-thinking characters.

Perhaps it was this: that at the time we were receiving the

dregs of a prejudice which had been developed in a previous generation against "yellow journalism"; and that our pulps were the lineal descendants of a long line of lower-class literature, much of it salacious, all of it beneath the attention of the better element.

For our pulps were no instant phenomenon of the period, but, instead, the outgrowth of a fiction form now over one hundred and thirty years old.

When titles for paperback books hawked by chapmen who peddled shoelaces and pincushions still ran to such intriguing lengths as: *The Affecting History of Sally Williams; afterwards Tippling Sally. Shewing how she left her father's house to follow an officer, who seduced her; and how she took to drinking, and at last became a vile prostitute, died in a hospital and was dissected by the surgeons. Tending to shew the pernicious effects of dram drinking,* there was an experiment begun in a more flexible medium for popular reading than the books—the newspaper. When all the available news was quickly and easily disposed of in a page or two, it was natural that other attractions be used to fill space. Fictional narratives were, accordingly, tried, with instantaneous success.

The outgrowth of this was the family Story Paper, an institution which persisted until the turn of this century. The story papers secured and kept readership by offering "plenty of sensation and no philosophy," as Robert Bonner—publisher of one of the most famous and long-lived of the publications—described their approach. In the guise of uplifting and edifying the public about conditions at large, these pre-pulpsters gleefully exploited the seamy and vice-ridden side of life.

Fanny H—— or *The Hunchback and the Roue* was a typical serial. It capitalized on popular interest in 1847 in a current
murder trial, that of one Richard P. Robinson who had been
accused of slaying the prostitute Ellen Jewett. To herald the
beginning of this saga, the publisher announced that it would
encompass:

> From the commencement of the life of his victim to the tragical
> termination of it, from the beginning of her life to its dishonorable
> issue, there is presented a singular history of innocence and trust-
> fulness, vice and crime . . . to illustrate the progressive steps of the
> career of the young and erring female, from her childhood to her
> sad assassination and to unfold the cause which led a young man,
> morally educated, to commit the greatest crime. . . .

Naturally, in dwelling on the 'cause which led a young man,
morally educated' to commit the big *faux pas,* there would
have to be a revelation of the life and habits of those gay blades
who consorted with ladies of the night, together with clinical
descriptions of the evils to which innocent girls may fall. . . .

It was but a step from fictionalizing the lives of actual
people to the creation of fictional beings who would be passed
off as real. The Old Sleuth, who first appeared in *The Fireside
Companion* in 1872, was the direct sire of all the thousand
private eyes whose legal depradations have flourished in print,
on the air and on the screen ever since. He was thought for
many years to be a genuine living person, but when his creators
began running as many as three different installment-adven-
tures in each weekly paper, the public caught on. No mere
human could possibly accomplish in one lifetime the deeds at-
tributed to the Old Sleuth.

Prior to the venerable detective's appearance, story papers leaned heavily on everyday romances, ghost stories, foreign intrigue and other figments of the hack-stable's imagination. The Grand Reunion—wherein all the principals are united in one orgy of who-is-who discovery—was the climax of most of these epics. In *Villains Galore,* Mary Noel describes one of the greatest triumphs of the Grand Reunion theme, Mrs. Southworth's *The Hidden Hand:*

In the story itself, Capitola (the heroine) was a rescued person from the very moment of her birth. A colored woman, who had been blindfolded by mysterious criminals, served as midwife at the birth of twins—a stillborn boy and the unexpected Capitola, who was smuggled away by the nurse at the mother's request, after the dead boy had been handed over to the criminals who were waiting in another room. The colored woman and the baby were later caught by the criminals and sold into slavery, but the ship on which they were carried away was wrecked and all hands lost except Capitola and her nurse who were rescued by one Herbert Grayson. Years later, when the nurse had died after making a deposition, Major Warfield of Virginia went to search for Capitola in New York and ran into her accidentally on his first landing. When he put up at a hotel, who should drop in that night but Herbert Grayson, who proved not only to be the long-lost son of Major Warfield's estranged sister, but also the devoted friend of a supposed widow who turned out later in the story to be really the wife of Major Warfield. He wrongly believed her unfaithful because of a trick played by a defeated rival for her hand. This Marah Rocke, whose marriage had been secret, had always gone by her maiden name; so that her son Traverse, born after the sudden desertion, was unknown to his father. Traverse soon became engaged to the rich and beautiful Clara Day, whose father met with sudden death just in time to leave Clara in the guardianship of her dead mother's half-brother Gabriel Le Noir, who also happened to be Capitola's nearest relative and rightful guardian, the brother of her rich murdered father. [Those who mourn the passing of plot in narrative fiction are advised to continue; others are permitted to skip.]

Capitola, who had been taken under Major Warfield's protection, was meanwhile the object of various abduction attempts on the part of numerous villains and rescues on the part of one hero, Herbert Grayson. Among other adventures, Capitola insisted on going to Gabriel Le Noir's Hidden House where Clara Day had been imprisoned and threatened with a fate that was worse than death as an alternative to marriage with Gabriel's son Craven. On the day when the forced marriage was scheduled, Capitola changed clothes with Clara, veiled herself heavily and was borne away to a church in the middle of the forest. Just as the priest reached the binding words, just as Capitola flung back her veil to stop the ceremony, just as Craven Le Noir sprang upon her, a blow from Herbert Grayson who was coming home unexpectedly on the way to the Mexican War and had stopped to inquire his way at the forest church, struck Craven Le Noir to the ground.

The frustrated guardian went off to the Mexican War where he found himself the colonel of a regiment containing not only Herbert Grayson but Traverse who had arrived from St. Louis where he had been practicing medicine. A cooked-up court martial failed and Traverse was honorably discharged. At home in Virginia, Capitola responded to the emergency of war by rescuing herself for a while. Traverse, as a doctor in New Orleans, one thousand miles from home, ran into Capitola's long-lost mother, who had been imprisoned in an insane asylum after her long concealment in the Hidden House back in Virginia. Gabriel Le Noir, meanwhile, died of wounds received at Mexico City and left behind him a packet of intercepted letters between Traverse and Clara, as well as a long overdue confession. In this he revealed himself as the murderer of his brother (Capitola's father), the abductor of the infant Capitola and the unsuccessful plotter against Marah Rocke's virtue. This confession was mailed to Major Warfield who was then satisfied of his wife's innocence. A Grand Reunion followed of:

1. Husband and wife: i.e., Marah Rocke and Major Warfield
2. Father and son: Traverse Rocke and Major Warfield
3. Lovers estranged by intercepted letters: Clara and Traverse
4. Mother and daughter: Capitola and Mrs. Eugene Le Noir
5. Rescued and rescuer: Capitola and Herbert Grayson. Since their previous marriage had been kept secret, Marah Rocke and Major Warfield had an excuse to be married again publicly, making a grand triple wedding to end the whole affair.

With such steady fare, it is small wonder that the story-paper works of fiction were deemed fit only for backstairs maids and idlers; although it may be observed that if they could follow the plots of those thrillers, they must have been of a high—or at least unique—order of intelligence.

No such cleverness was required for full appreciation of the next development in pulp fiction, Buffalo Bill. With his appearance, the younger generation of boys—untempted by romantic triple weddings—began to devour the story papers; and a tradition was born. General disapproval was followed by pulpit blasts, confiscation, hide-tannings and stern talkings-to. But the kids had found a hero.

Buffalo Bill is inextricably entwined with the legend of his creator, Ned Buntline, otherwise known as Edward Zane Carroll Judson, whose real life was far more fraught with peril and adventure than William Cody's ever was.

Judson: ran away to sea at the age of eleven; served in the Seminole War in Florida; was lynched by an incensed mob in Nashville, Tennessee, after he'd killed a jealous husband in a duel; escaped the lynching when the rope broke; organized a riot in New York City and was jailed for a year; fought with the Union army in the Civil War, emerging as a Colonel with twenty bullets in his body; then went West to roam the untamed land with Wild Bill Hickok, Texas Jack and a youngster named William Frederick Cody.

Cody wore his golden hair at shoulder length, sported a goatee, fringed jacket and wide-brimmed cowboy hat, and was altogether the living prototype for the fictional Western hero Ned Buntline had in mind. Assisted by Cody's grandiloquent tales of hunting expeditions and Indian battles, plus a recounting of his ceaseless efforts to avenge the death of his father in the Bloody Kansas struggle, Buntline started the most popular series of stories America had ever seen. Not that E. Z. C. Judson was a tyro seeking inspiration. He was, at the time of his Know-Nothing party riot in New York, one of the best-paid writers in the world. But his own experiences were, so he thought, commonplace. He was certain that realistic yarns of the new frontier would eclipse any personal reminiscences he could get into print. So he went West in search of a hero, and found Buffalo Bill.

The great cowboy's saga began irresistibly, setting a style from which expert pulpsters seldom varied:

Ned Buntline's Great Story!!
BUFFALO BILL

The King of the Border Men!
The wildest and truest story
I ever wrote.
By Ned Buntline (E. Z. C. Judson)
Chapter I

An oasis of green wood on a Kansas prairie—a bright stream shining like liquid silver in the moonlight—a log house built under the limbs of great trees—within this home a happy group. This is my first picture.

Look well upon the leading figure in that group. You will see him but once, yet on his sad fate hinges all the wild and fearful realities which are to follow, drawn to a very great extent, not from imagination but from life itself. . . .

Buntline goes on to describe the family at its evening devotions. Then, suddenly, there is the sound of hoofbeats. A cry: "Hallo—the house!" Father Cody opens the door. He is greeted by the jeers of Southern sympathizers and the taunts of Colonel M'Kandlas—who levels his pistol and fires! Father Cody, good husband and outstanding Christian, clutches at his chest and falls dead before his horrified family. Then:

"If them gals was a little older—but never mind, boys, this will be a lesson for the sneaks that come upon the border—let's be off, for there's plenty more work to do before daylight!" continued the wretch, turning the head of his horse to ride away.

"Stop!"

It was but a single word—spoken, too, by a boy whose blue eyes shone wildly in a face as white as new-fallen snow and full as cold—spoken as he stood erect over the body of his dead father, weaponless and alone.

Yet that ruffian, aye, and all of his mad wreckless crew, stopped as if a mighty spell was laid upon them.

"You, Jake M'Kandlas, have murdered my father! You, base cowards, who saw him do this dark deed, spoke no word to restrain him. I am only Little Bill, his son, but as God in Heaven hears me now I will kill every father's son of you before the beard grows on my face!"

"Little Bill" soon became big Bill, and in weekly installments held the nation captive as he sought vengeance, killed buffalo, scouted the plains, led the Cavalry to victory after victory, and dueled with the bravest Indian Chiefs. He was the bravest man on earth and the most exciting figure in all literature—to small-fry, anyway. What kid with the trace of an imagination could fail to respond to such action-filled lines as:

" 'Then come on, you red devil, and have it out!' shouted Buffalo Bill, and, forgetting General Merritt's orders not to expose himself, he dashed at full speed toward the Chief who, likewise, with a wild yell, rode toward him."?

Answer: No kid, regardless of age. As Quentin Reynolds comments in his estimable *The Fiction Factory:*

Buffalo Bill with his inevitable Winchester barking for law and order, became a permanent fixture not only in American fiction but in American folklore. He was undoubtedly the most indestructible character in all fiction. The public couldn't get enough of Buffalo Bill. The stories were translated into every language and were just as popular in foreign countries.

When Buntline/Judson died, the *New York Weekly* assigned Colonel Prentiss Ingraham to carry on the series. The Colonel was a natural fighter. He became a lieutenant at eighteen in Lee's army and, when the South ran out of territory to lose to the Yankees, he set out for Mexico to join the army headed by Juárez. Later he turned up in the Austrian army, fighting against the Russians and the Turks, in Africa and in Asia. After escaping from the Spanish, he headed West where he met Cody, Hickok and Buntline, and launched into a career of writing. Within a short time, his stories about scout Pawnee Bill were very nearly as popular as Buntline's material.

Ingraham was once asked by an interviewer how he got his plots. The Colonel replied, "Well, I open up with action and then just go ahead and write. I begin, 'Crack! Crack! Crack! Three more redskins bit the dust.' From there on it's easy."

Invariably Ingraham, like Buntline before him, would put Buffalo Bill in a situation of great peril, and then extricate him through his own reckless bravery or with the help of a loyal Indian ally [reports Reynolds, a keen student of pulpdom's great history]. Improbabilities never bothered either of these two facile men. Their own careers were studded with improbable and even impossible situations and escapades.

Under Colonel Ingraham's aegis, Buffalo Bill continued for years in the weekly papers with undiminished appeal.

Sensing, in the early part of this half-century, that Westerns had just about had it, Street & Smith—then, as always, the leading pulp publishers—began to think of other ways to tap the pockets of youngsters. Although entertainments were not omnipresent, as they are today, loose coin was in correspondingly short supply. Accordingly, it took a solid jolt on the cover of a magazine (the natural development of the story papers) and a substantial dose of interior escape to effect the transfer of a week's spending money from knickers to newsstand vendors.

Nick Carter was the answer.

He first appeared as the protégé of "Seth Parker, the old detective" (a not-too-subtle revival of the Old Sleuth) in a story written by John Russell Coryell. Ormond Smith, at that time head of the Street & Smith firm, liked the idea of a young detective, and assigned Frederick Van Rensselaer Dey to do a series featuring Nick Carter. It was an immediate sensation. Yellowed copies of *The Nick Carter Weekly* continue to fetch high prices.

The masthead of *The Nick Carter Weekly* portrayed a clean-cut collar-ad youth in the center of the page, surrounded by sketches of "Nick Carter in various disguises": A queued Chinese laborer; a monocled fop; a gray-haired grandmother; a straw-chewing, bearded rube; a top-hatted industrialist puffing a cigar; and a toothy Negro. It was plain that Carter was a master of the art of changing appearance. He carried paints, droopy mustaches and wigs at all times, and could become another person faster than Clark Kent turns into Superman. Unlike the private eye we know and respect in current literature, Nick disdained alcohol, tobacco and sex. Yet, in the true traditions of his craft, he encouraged the perpetration of mayhem upon his person, suffering as many head-cloutings, jaw-smashings, waylayings, dopings and maimings as his descendant, Mike Hammer.

When we consider that the writers who filled the pages of our favorite crime-laden paperbacks were brought up, most of them, on Nick Carter, we can understand the near inflexibility of the "stalwart, high-principled hero enmeshed in violent situations" formula. It carried the first recognizable private eye to peaks of popularity even higher than those attained by Buffalo Bill.

Most of the out-and-out sensationalism to which educators and clergymen objected in the nineteenth century was contained not in the Street & Smith pulps but in the physically similar "dime novels." Beadle & Adams, publishers, clothed their little publications in orange covers, but the content was usually "yellow."

Under this form one of America's best known, least talented and most fondly remembered authors made his mark. Horatio Alger, Jr., wrote 119 books (or, as a critic commented, "one book, rewritten 118 times") about poor boys who persevered throughout adversity and gained wealth and fame as their reward. There was nothing in these morality tales to shock the mildest country minister (indeed, Alger was a sometime Unitarian minister himself), yet they were frowned upon and, probably as a result, sold an almost unbelievable 250,000,000 copies.

In his college days, Alger was known as Holy Horatio, generally because of his starchy, abstemious nature and specifically because one night he refused to cooperate with his landlady, who had walked into his room stark naked and asked him to join her in a tango. A subsequent trip to Paris, however, fired him with worldly ideas and experiences—he wrote in his diary: "I was a fool to have waited so long. It is not nearly so vile as I had thought"—and he returned to the United States willing, if not downright eager, to sample earthly joys. Of course, as everyone knows who has ever brushed with his literary corpus, no trace of this moral liberation ever found its way into the Horatio Alger, Jr., books, except as illustrations of the evils young men must struggle to avoid. These illustrations gobbled up dimes from the nation's youth and were passed along in secret delight like so many pornographic pictures.

Alger's anemic but popular heroes were soon joined by *Tom Edison, Jr.,* a similarly chaste though somewhat more adventurous youth. His exploits were devoted to the apprehension of evildoers through the use of scientific methods and inventions, a presage of future trends. Of course they were wholly fictional, prepared by divers hands; yet they contributed heavily to the legendization of Edison himself, who, in spite of his significant discoveries, was known by his acquaintances to be the dullest, crankiest, most colorless and least legendary of men.

With the appearance of *Frank Merriwell,* the Street & Smith company assumed unchallenged leadership of the adventure-fiction market. Merriwell—a Yale student, as everyone knows; or, more properly, *the* Yale student—was created by Burt L. Standish (pen name of William Gilbert Patten) in the late 1890's. Standish's experience with the university he was to immortalize consisted of his attendance at a half-dozen football games and a single stroll around the campus; yet he made Yale so real and Merriwell so believable that enrollment at the college increased by hundreds.

The literary quality of these stories was regrettably low, though not so low as in the Alger and Tom Edison epics. The late George Jean Nathan actually claimed to enjoy them and often beat the drums for a return to those simple values. He regarded the absence of a Standish biography as the most glaring and insupportable omission in American literary history.

"His readers numbered millions," Nathan complained. "For one who read Mark Twain's *Huckleberry Finn* or *Tom Sawyer,* there were ten thousand who read Standish's *Frank Merriwell's Dilemma or The Rescue of Inza* and *Frank Merriwell at Yale or The Winning Last Quarter-Mile.* The little candy and cigar stores of that day, the chief distributing centers of the Standish *opera,* had longer lines of small boys with nickels in their hands every Friday than Barnum's or Forepaugh's circus could ever boast. . . ."

Pawnee Bill, John L., Jr., Clif Faraday of Annapolis, Mark Mallory of West Point and *Diamond Dick* were the heroes who followed Merriwell. They were uniformly antiseptic types, but they assumed a degree of importance to America's mass readership which no literary creation of recent times has been able to duplicate. For years they rode tall, shrugging off the bullets of wrongdoers and the slings and arrows of critics; but they could not defend themselves against their greatest enemy: Growing Sophistication. One by one they bit the dust. *Buffalo Bill* was the last to fall, and a sad day it was. He was laid to rest in 1919 and mourned on the masthead of the zippy, modern magazine that did him in.

It is that magazine—*Western Story Magazine*—Formerly *New Buffalo Bill Weekly*—which forms our direct link with the past.

For more than thirty years, *Western Story Magazine* (the Buffalo Bill subtitle was soon dropped) appeared twice a month. Most of us cut our teeth on it. While Soldiers of Fortune, Scientific Detectives and Yellow Menaces provided aperitif, appetizer and dessert, the changeless saga of the American West was our main course. Every kid on every block dreamed of being a sheriff, and "Cowboys" was the national game.

Thanks in large part to a moody, tortured genius called Frederick Schiller Faust. We didn't know him by that name. We knew Max Brand, George Owen Baxter, Martin Dexter, Evin Evans, David Manning, Peter Dawson, John Frederick, Pete Morland. But they were all Faust, the most incredibly prolific—and unquestionably the best—pulp writer in the business.

No man ever lived [said Quentin Reynolds] who could invent so many plots (not even Balzac) or so crowd a few thousand words with action as Max Brand [his most famous pseudonym]. No man since the days when Sir Walter Scott was turning out his Waverley Novels ever spewed forth so many words. He wrote about thirty million of them during his career, and most of them were words of action.

They weren't bad words, either; and though the plots were usually variations of the primitive Vengeance theme, they had —and have—an unaccountable freshness and vitality. Unaccountable, that is, until one recalls that Brand/Faust had the instincts, if not the skill, of a serious author. For pulp fiction in general, and his own in particular, he had supreme contempt. He never read over his first drafts. He never saw the magazines in which his work appeared; indeed, the first rule of his house was that no adventure magazine of any description would be tolerated on the premises. He genuinely hated "Max Brand" and the rest of the pseudonymous stable. Yet he was the absolute master of the craft, and of every other form of writing except that which he most respected. At serious prose and poetry he was, fortunately for us and tragically for him, a failure. His occasional slim volumes, published under his real name, were mostly attic-scented, bloodless, pedestrian, worthless. And he knew it, and it broke his heart.

Tiring of the pulps' low pay, Brand moved on to the slicks where he was equally successful. Warner Brothers paid him $3,000 a week. M-G-M gave him a fortune for creating Dr. Kildare (currently a television series). He made more money than any other writer of that period, yet he was consistently broke. "It costs me $70,000 a year just to survive," he commented at a time when $4,000 was considered a good annual wage.

Of course, his readers knew nothing of this. While we wrote in angry letters to editors, complaining that George Owen Baxter was a bum and why didn't they print more stuff by Max Brand, nonetheless we sensed a superiority about the Faust product. His self-despised stories in *Western Story, Black Mask, Argosy, Adventure* and *Blue Book* entertained millions and attracted a coterie of enthusiasts who published mimeographed booklets in praise of their idol. No other pulpster seemed to have Brand's flair for melodrama or his ability to create an authentic setting. The illusion of reality was his finest trick. In an extraordinary blend of crude machine-gun prose and adjective-studded poetry, he could conjure up Asia with a yak-skin tent, tethered Mongolian ponies and a fur-capped khan, all so vivid that one could smell the dung-fire smoke and shiver in the icy blasts that swept down off the Khanga Mountains.

Faust became a legend in his time, a figure from one of Brand's most perfervid adventures. Seeking refuge from his disappointment, he became an alcoholic and, in 1938, was sent to Italy to die. Instead of dying, he fell in love with the country and developed into one of its champion tennis players. He took up horseback riding. He bought an Isotta-Fraschini and earned the sobriquet, "The Fast American." But all the while, he continued to crank out his pulp fiction. He had to. Compelled to find an excuse for the failure that, he knew, would eventually crush him, he bought a palatial villa in Florence, staffed it with servants and tutors, and kept his standard of living stratospherically high. He was still the King of the Pulps when the war broke out. Deeply affected, and yearning for some *real* adventure, Faust—aged fifty-two—managed to talk the American army into giving him a set of war-correspondent credentials. His first assignment, on the front lines, was his last. Fifth man over the top, he was cut down by enemy fire; and so he died, clutching an olive branch, in the Italian hills he loved.

By a mysterious coincidence, the pulps themselves began to cough out their life at about this time, as though the passing of their king had left them blind and weak and unable to survive.

We heard no death-knell. As we stretched out on the lawn swing with a copy of *Spicy Detective Stories,* we heard only the *whisssk-whisssk-whisssk* of the rotating lawn sprinklers, the distant rumble of streetcars and a voice crying *"Ole ole ocean freeeee!"* And, of course, Dan Turner's gun, sneezing *kachow-kachow!* The world was a small, quiet place for most of us then, and it was for that reason, as much as for any other, that we escaped into the vast, noisy world of the pulps.

They were at the crest of their popularity just before and during the war years. Hundreds of titles offered an almost unbelievable variety of reading experiences to the American teen-ager, and most were well within the boundaries of good taste—the same boundaries over which our television networks leap, like demented impalas, every hour of every day in this age.

It must be admitted, however, that only those who actually bothered to read the magazines could be expected to understand this. Their physical appearance suggested nothing short of mortal sin. Something about the quality of the paper—so exciting to kids—summoned up, for adults, visions of brothels, public toilets, French postcards and petty crime. The illustrations, generally of a low order of craftsmanship, depicted scenes of extreme violence. But it was the covers, more than anything else, that turned the grown-up world against the pulps. To say that they were lurid is to say that the Atlantic Ocean is wet. They were—and this, also, is a weak descriptive word—fantastic. In a way unknown to me, and unduplicated by artists in any other field, those masters of the brush managed to work sex, action, horror, terror, beauty, ugliness, virtue, sin and a dozen other elements, into every picture they painted. Their goal was to tempt the newsstand browser into parting with cash, and this goal they achieved with complete success. But they achieved a great deal more. Most pulp addicts were foxy enough to know that the cover of a magazine seldom bore the slightest connection to the fiction it was supposed to illustrate, that, indeed, the "backs" were simply come-ons for saps and suckers; yet we revered those pulp artists and regarded their contribution, and their position, as being equal to those of the writers.

Consider a typical *Spicy Detective Stories* cover. This rich *oeuvre* portrayed a leggy blonde whose pink-and-white skin was so dewy-fresh as to be palpable. Clad only in ripped black-lace panties, she clutched another garment to her meticulously rendered, melon-heavy breasts, concealing little of either. Her face was a mask of fear, and with good reason: a blue-black automatic thrust toward her like a finger of doom.

Needless to say, no such scene was to be encountered in the lead story (titillatingly titled *Murder in the Harem*). In the classic "dirty magazine," confiscated on sight by all parents and custodians, sex was treated with the slightly leering but profound innocence of the neighborhood know-it-all. The authors, chief among them Robert Leslie Bellem, larded their narratives with suggestive dialogue and took care to describe "her silk-clad, lissome body," "a flash of white thigh," "breasts straining at their silken prison," etc., but the truth is that a diet of reading restricted to *Spicy Detective Stories* would do nothing to dissuade one from belief in the theory of the stork. The same holds for such other "legendary" pulps as *Spicy Western, Spicy Adventure* and *Breezy Tales*. They were not so much read as examined, or searched, for "hot parts"; and if the editors had been thoughtful enough to print the mildly erotic sections in a different color, they would have saved us all a lot of time.

There were three genuinely erotic pulp magazines, but their disguises were so excellent that the authorities didn't catch on for months. *Horror Stories, Terror Tales* and *Marvel Tales* would all curl your hair, even today. Ostensibly science fiction/supernatural publications, they packed more honest perversion into one page than one could find in Tijuana's most notorious Den of Iniquity. Plain, ordinary, garden-variety sex was eschewed. In its place, we were given flagellation, sadism, orgies, homosexuality, pederasty and a host of diversions which popped the eyes from the sweaty heads of teen-agers throughout the country. A typical story concerned the evil mistress of a castle who, out of ennui, staged impressive parties, during which she would drug her guests, take them to a dungeon, clap them in irons and torture them to death. Lush young girls were stripped naked, after which operation their hostess would approach with a branding iron and burn the nipples from their breasts.

Our attention to these magazines could fairly be described as rapt; however, they perished in due course, and I believe we were all just a bit relieved.

Relief did not attend the passing, though, of our legitimate friends. *Argosy*—the *Argosy* of the six-part serials, of Zagat and Verrill and Brand, of Mongol hordes and incredible sea voyages—staggered on awhile, then turned into a slick; and we mourned. We knew that the quality would vanish. Instinctively we sensed the truth of Ray Bradbury's maxim: "The pulps were alive, they had texture, they breathed; the slicks were born with their pores closed, they couldn't breathe, they were dead." Doc Savage left us. The Shadow disappeared. One by one, the great magazines ceased publication.

The last survivors were the best and the favorites: the science-fiction and fantasy magazines. They had everything the other pulps had, and more. The grand old advertisements were there. Sherwin Cody counseled us to speak better English from the pages of *Amazing Stories*. We continued to read of the near-tragedies averted by the use of Eveready flashlight batteries. The kindly, gray-haired man who proclaimed, "I talked with God! Yes, I did—actually and literally!" was with us; we could still Find Out Today how we could train at home to become radio technicians; we could buy Beautiful Lifelike Photo Rings, Learn Music as Easy as A-B-C, grace our faces with good-looking glasses for $2.95, insure our whole family for $1.00 a month, cure our piles with Page's Pile Tablets, or join the Rosicrucians and learn the Mysteries of Life.

Most important, we could still thrill to high adventure—in a day when adventure was becoming suspect—with the wonderful space operas offered by most of the publications. For the Junior Scientists and Astronauts among us, there was *Astounding Science Fiction,* a no-nonsense magazine featuring the extrapolations of such sober and serious men as A. E. Van Vogt, Robert Heinlein, John W. Campbell, Lester del Rey and George O. Smith. For the rest of us, either too young or too unsophisticated—or perhaps insufficiently bright—to enjoy *Astounding,* there were *Amazing Stories, Fantastic Adventures, Startling Stories, Thrilling Wonder Stories, Super Science, Stirring Science, Captain Future, Unknown Worlds, Weird Tales,* and—for the real, dyed-in-the-wool pulp hounds—*Planet Stories,* which featured Westerns, pirate sagas and Viking tales, all set on planets other than earth. The heavies in *Planet* were invariably "BEMs" (Bug-Eyed Monsters), the girls invariably "lush" or "generously proportioned," the heroes invariably "bronzed and muscular," the prose invariably atrocious and exciting.

Amazing and its sister publication *Fantastic Adventures* led the field, with *Startling* and *Thrilling Wonder* close behind. Such was the appeal of their product that thousands of kids formed fan clubs, issued mimeographed and hectographed magazines, and developed into a vast but highly insular phenomenon known as *Sf-fandom.* To belong, one had merely to be something of a nut, so membership was all but unlimited. The object of *Sf-fandom* was avowedly the dissemination of inside information about and the glorification of science fiction, but in actuality it was a correspondence club for social misfits, most of whom devoted more time to the reading of letters from fellow fans, or *fen,* than to the professional magazines. It gave teen-agers a rare and exciting sense of *belonging* and from its ragtag ranks have come many of today's most successful authors and scientists, so it may be judged to have been one of the happier outgrowths of the pulp craze.

The authors we venerated, when we were not corresponding with new friends, were of a vanished breed: the loving hacks. They wrote for money (averaging two cents per word in the *sf* heyday), but it was not their only goad. Pulpsters like Edmond Hamilton, Leigh Brackett, Don Wilcox, David Wright O'Brian, William P. McGivern, Henry Kuttner, Robert Bloch, August Derleth, William Lawrence Hamling, Ray Palmer and Manley Wade Wellman wrote pulp fiction primarily because they had a hell of a good time doing it; and however the quality of their stories might have varied, the enthusiasm with which they set those stories down remained consistently high. Whether they wrote of X-ray spectacles or time travel or beast kings of Jupiter, they wrote with genuine gusto.

Until 1950.

1950 may be taken, loosely, as the year the pulps gave their last kick. A few lingered on, twitching, then they, too, expired, and the pulps became another odd part of our heritage—fondly remembered, frequently recalled, in spirit form, by millions of ex-kids who never asked to grow out of those summer twilights.

It is easy to sneer at those crumbling yellow magazines, and at the people responsible for them; but we should salute, instead, for we owe the pulps an incalculable debt of gratitude. They stimulated, prodded and jostled our young minds; they broadened our narrow horizons; they gave us a splendid outlet for our natural pent-up violence. Though attacked as propagators of delinquency, it is doubtful that the pulps ever led so much as one youngster astray; indeed, a glance at the criminal records of the day will reveal that the true delinquents seldom read anything but the fine print on cigarette packages. Parents' forebodings notwithstanding, the pulps helped us in many ways, strengthened and comforted us, led us to an appreciation of literature and prepared us, if not for life, then at least for dreams.

Now they are gone, echoed dimly in the novels of Ian Fleming, their corpses dancing grotesquely in the flickering light of the television tube, but, truly, gone, and forever. Nor can they be brought back.

Still . . . if you listen very hard, very late at night, perhaps you will hear, distantly, the clang of swords, the drum of hoofs, the rush of rockets and the spine-chilling laugh of a man they called the Shadow. I know I do.

There's nothing
to be afraid of
my child

THE AMUSEMENT of yesterday's amusement parks was compounded of joy, excitement, awe and fear. Today's parks provide all but the last, and the omission is unfortunate.

It may be that Franklin Roosevelt was turning more than a phrase when he said, "The only thing we have to fear is fear itself." We certainly fear it now. Having learned what the word trauma means, we have decided to protect our children, presumably to make sure they won't turn out like us. It is natural and proper to protect them from danger, disease and death, but I question the wisdom of protecting them from nightmares. No one has proved yet that the effect of nightmares is deleterious, nor have psychologists argued that the early conquest of fear is anything but helpful. Yet we seem to think it is a bad thing. With the niggling exception of a possible thermonuclear cataclysm, we have given them nothing to be afraid of.

Terror was a condition sought after avidly a

generation ago, and nowhere was it found so quickly as at an amusement park. If one ran with a pack, as one usually did, it was, sooner or later, necessary to take a ride on a roller coaster. There were kids who claimed to be unafraid of those mile-high rockets, but most of us were petrified of them. We would stand at the base and look up at the frail spider-web structure of wooden struts; we would watch a train of cars climbing slowly, ratchets clicking a death march, slowly, at an impossible angle, up and up to the very summit, poising there an eternal moment, tipping, then roaring straight down, out of control, a hundred miles an hour, to certain doom, as the passengers shrieked good-bye; and, watching this, and imagining ourself in one of those cars, we felt the dryness of the throat and the wetness of the armpits and the hammering of the heart that are terror. But that was only a presage of what we felt when we took our place in line for the Bobs, or the Blue Streak, or the Silver Flash. Then we knew, without question, that we were going to perish. We'd heard stories of how sometimes those cars had ripped loose from their tracks and gone crashing into the park, killing hundreds, if not thousands. Yet we couldn't show our fear, although of course we did, every time we shrugged and chuckled and said, "Nothin' to it!" It became terror mixed with indecision. While in line, one could always bolt. It was possible to get out of it. All you had to do was say, "I'd prefer not to ride today," and walk away. But you never did. The guys would laugh, and you would spend the rest of your life remembering this cowardice. So you stayed in the line. Better to die sitting down than live on your knees.

Once past the turnstile, the feeling changed again. Now it

was terror mixed with resignation. No getting out of it now.

Breathing in quick, short breaths, we listened to the far-off screams and tried to think of the fine meal we were going to have at the hot-dog stand afterward. A wait of five hours, surely, and we became convinced that the ride had shut down for the day. "Sorry, boys, no more rides!" Then, with a wild, sinister clacking, the cars appeared. The passengers looked green. You could almost smell their sweat.

"Everybody in!"

And then it became pure, undistilled terror.

We got in with our sickly smile, pulled the grab bar down tight upon our lap, and addressed ourself silently to God, although we wouldn't have blamed Him for not listening to us. It was our own fault. We got ourself into this. We didn't have the sense to say no in the first place. We could have. Nobody could make us do anything we didn't——

"Here we go!"

And the terror increased with every turn of the wheels. Now we were the ones being watched from below, the madmen who were risking their lives.

It took forever to reach the top. We sat there, smile rigid and aching, knees trembling, and we tried to squeeze the metal bar in half. When we saw the summit approaching, we closed our eyes tight.

The suspended moment, high above the park, above the people, above the sensible rides, and, finally, the incredible locomotive-thundering downward plunge. We couldn't breathe. We couldn't think. We couldn't feel. It was the end of the world.

But then the cars arced upwards again, and we dared to open our eyes, astonished to be alive. Another, shorter plunge, and up, and around, and down again, and up, and the end, not of the world, but of the ride.

And we got out weakly and walked to the hot-dog stand and thought about our courage.

"How'd ya like it?"

"It was fun."

And we went home feeling like heroes.

Not, however, before visiting the fun houses. They were endless black caverns through which you had to move carefully, and bravely, else you would be lost forever. We entered joking, always, but the jokes soon turned to whispers.

"A guy was killed here a few years ago. My uncle told me. He was cut up with a knife."

"Who by?"

"They never found out."

"Maybe he's still in here. It'd be a perfect place to hide."

"Aah, that's nutty. How'd he get anything to eat?"

"Simple. He stays in all day, then he goes out at night and robs the hot-dog stands."

"I smell hot dogs."

"You got one in your hand."

"What was that?"

"What?"

"Wait a second, don't move anybody. Can't 'cha hear that breathing?"

"Nah."

"I heard breathing."

"You're just trying to scare everybody."

"Honest!"

Through the corridors, bumping knees against out-jutting obstructions, walking into walls, ending in cul-de-sacs, retracing, all by feel in the dank, sea-and-hot-dog–smelling blackness, circling back, continuing, ascending ladders to nowhere, falling through trap doors, tumbling on the padded leather below, passing the Crazy Room, the Mirror Room, the Upside-down room, and, turning a corner, walking smack into a man in the act of butchering a woman in a bathtub. The waxwork gallery of famous murderers. Landru, Dr. Crippin, Jack the Ripper, all staring hungrily at us, eyes ablaze.

"D'ja see him move?"

"Yes! Oh, God! Oh, God! Let's get outta here!"

"Afternoon, boys."

"Aah, it's a trick. He just works here."

"How do ya know?"

Off, away, out, through the corridors again, down the slide, and, blinking, into the sunlight.

Heroes all, except perhaps at night, asleep, when we sat beside Jack the Ripper in the first car of the roller coaster, which parted from the tracks in a horrible shower of sparks and flew into the air, twisting over and over, while Jack laughed and raised his knife.

Now we have Disneyland. It is a splendidly imaginative park, full of wonders to behold, but it offers no terrors to the young. Walt Disney, who always made sure there was at least one spine-chilling sequence in his films, has turned Pollyanna, perhaps in response to the letters of worried parents. His films are all sunlight and fun, now, and so is his park, like all the other new ones. But life isn't like that. It contains sunlight and fun, to be sure, but it also contains shadows and terrors. And that we are able to cope with these things is due, I believe, to the fact that fear was a staple in our diet.

Good Lord,

it's alive!

AN IMPORTANT conference was held not long ago
in the New York executive offices of 20th Century-
Fox. Under discussion was a new title for a recently completed Western movie. A Dorothy
Parker devotee had come up with *Enough Rope,*
but the Powers said no. Not enough B.O. appeal.
Insufficient bazazz. "It lays there." Other titles
followed: *Rope Law, The Hell-Bent Kid, Fast
Draw at Fort Smith, Quick Draw at Fort Smith,*
and, finally, just plain *Quick Draw.* Charlie Einfeld, Fox's Eastern publicity chief, shook his head.
"Westerns," he said, "are doing lousy business.
Can't we get something a little flashier?"

A few more How-abouts followed, then a
nameless assistant snapped his fingers. "How
about—*The Fiend Who Walked the West?*" he
suggested.

An awed and respectful silence, of the type
usually reserved for births, deaths, treaties and
decisions of international importance, fell upon
the little group. Cigars were removed slowly
from mouths. Smiles replaced worried frowns.

"That," said Einfeld, at last, "is a million-dollar idea."

He was wrong. It was, if we are to believe the trade papers, a two-million-dollar idea. The phony title, together with an equally phony ad campaign (which turned handsome ladies' wear executive Robert Evans into a monster by means of painting him green and giving him Orphan Annie eyeballs), allowed the producers to palm off a routine Western as a horror movie. And there is no surer road to success in Hollywood today.

Horror—a category understood by exhibitors and audiences to include science fiction, fantasy, the weird and supernatural, and even psychological suspense dramas—is the biggest thing in the entertainment business. It has been the biggest thing in the entertainment business for nearly five years. Far from faltering, as everyone predicted it would do, it has gained steadily in strength and is going stronger than ever. In 1957, fifty-two horror films were made. In 1958, seventy-five. Over *one hundred* full-length features were issued during the 1959 season. And the success of American-International (*House of Usher, Premature Burial, The Raven*) suggests that very soon horror will account for over *one third* of all U.S. motion-picture output.

Which means that horror is now one of the basic American commodities, like breakfast cereal and soap. In terms of finances, it is bigger business than the whole of hard-cover book publishing. In fact, if a single concern controlled all the merchandise, that concern would be considered a blue-chip stock. As it is, the only independent motion picture enterprises for which banks will advance "second money" are those with name stars or "monster quickies." In either case, a satisfactory return is assured; any other type of project is considered risky.

Hollywood's major studios are still largely owned and operated by septuagenarians who can afford to live in the past. These elderly men, whose incredible lack of foresight allowed the vast potential of television to fall to the radio broadcasters, do not take the horror cycle seriously. They ignore it on the theory that it must therefore go away. But as other American industries have moved inexorably from scatterings of small manufacturers to virtual monopolies, the movie business—which consisted of five studios at its peak—has been drawing steadily closer to the capitalistic ideal of Much Profit for Many. Not too long ago an "independent producer" was simply someone out of a job. Today there are over one thousand independent producers, mostly young men, and if it weren't necessary for them—and their television counterparts—to rent space and facilities for their numerous productions, it is unlikely that the once powerful "majors" would even exist today. And if, in turn, it weren't for the staple of horror, these independents would probably not be thriving as they are. Thus, paradoxically, it can be said that the big companies, to whom the subject is faintly odious, owe their very lives to the public's new-found taste for horror.

That taste, we can now observe, is apparently insatiable. Musical crazes, such as the twist, spring into strange and fiery birth, threaten to incinerate the world, then flicker out. Crazes in art, fashion, design, even in literature, are calculated to the same fragile mortality. But occasionally a craze, seemingly no different from others, hangs on. Instead of dying, it grows more vigorous. And no amount of public outcry or litigation can hurt it. Such a phenomenon is horror. It has always been with us, but never in such quantity as now, never as a real genre.

It is time—almost past time—for an evaluation. What accounts for the sudden, immense popularity of "creature-features"? Who makes them? Who goes to see them? What, if any, sociological and psychological significance is to be found in the trend?

A definition of terms would seem in order before we begin. The horror film per se, in its purest and most acceptable form, consists of certain standard ingredients, and is as formalized as a Hoot Gibson Western or a classical ballet. Of cardinal importance, as we shall see later, is the presence of a monster (n. 1. a fabulous animal compounded of brute and human shape or of the shapes of various brutes, as a centaur, a griffin, or a sphinx. 2. an animal or a plant of abnormal form or structure, as from marked malformation, the absence of certain parts or organs, etc. 3. something unnatural or monstrous. 4. a person that excites horror, as by wickedness, cruelty, etc. 5. any animal or thing of huge size). This monster, preferably man-made—though extraterrestrials seem to be getting a tendril in the door—must be, either consciously or unconsciously, a menace. It must be ugly as hell, at least twice as strong as ten healthy men, and awkward. No one knows exactly why, but there has never been a successful monster which did not stagger, shamble, lumber, or crawl.

The second ingredient for the classic horror film is the mad, or misguided, professor. Generally in his late twenties or early thirties, and handsome to a fault, he either Creates the

Creature or Lets It In, or, as in latter-day productions, Turns into It. He ought to be basically likable though inclined to a certain bookish attitude, which annoys and frustrates the third ingredient: Beauty. Beauty, who must combine the qualities of the girl next door and the star performer at a Moroccan bagnio, is either the World's Foremost Authority on Phytogenesis or, simply, a Good Friend.

At some point in the picture, it is necessary for Beauty to be threatened by the Monster and for the Professor to save her. Shortly afterward, the earth itself must stand in peril of its existence, and the Professor must, in collaboration with the army or by himself, rout the Menace.

That is the basic mixture; but even the garnishments have become ritualized. Dialogue, for example, is machined so that the parts are interchangeable. In each horror film you will almost certainly hear: (*Assistant to Professor*) "You must stop these monstrous experiments before it is too late!" Or (*again the Assistant*): "There are some things best left to God!" Or (*the Professor, to himself*): "Good Lord, it's alive!" And a horror flick without "You call me mad! [insane chuckling] That is what they said of Galileo, of Newton, yes, even of Einstein! I tell you, mankind will *worship* me for my madness!" is unthinkable.

The formula is a dangerous thing to monkey with, Hollywood has found, for it is the backbone of this new multimillion-dollar business. When a producer tries to cash in on the craze while attempting something a little different (as Walter Wanger did some years ago with *The Body Snatchers*), he runs a risk. He may do all right or he may find that variations on the theme are both costlier and more difficult than the standard melody. Besides, no one asked him for originality.

In this respect, as, surprisingly, in others, the horror field may be compared to that of the Western. The Western has its own narrow and inflexible set of rules, and no one in his right mind would try to break them. Bend them a bit, yes— but never break them. Even *High Noon* had, in addition to its subtle overtones, the classic treatment; and the much touted *Shane* might have been written by Owen Wister. Good or bad, old or new, the Western contains a Hero, a Heroine, a Villain, and a Fight. Put chaps and a ten-gallon hat on the Professor, give the Scarey a black horse, and switch the scene from Alamogordo to Tombstone, and you have very nearly the same thing.

When Universal-International was grinding out horror films in 1956, a studio spokesman was quoted as saying, "We're still making Westerns." He then pointed out that the monster movies were using music from old "oaters," which accounted for "a considerable savings."

This—the economic element—is, of course, a big factor in the craze. It was discovered a few years ago that people were going to horror films as a *habit*. With rare exceptions, no picture was preferred over another, so long as certain ingredients were promised. And whereas Westerns had to go to the expense of at least one recognizable star, it appeared that no one paid any attention to the human actors in creature films: the monster was, and is, a sufficient draw. (According to Steve Broidy, head of Allied Artists, "It doesn't have to be a fancy monster, or expensive, or even particularly well done. Just about anything will do, *provided it's on-screen a lot.*") Thus it became possible for under-capitalized independent groups to make pictures for absurdly low figures. The average "cheap" quickie-Western at Universal-International cost $500,000 in the early fifties; the average horror film is brought in for substantially less than $100,000, counting everything. In some cases, the costs and profits are shocking. Bert I. Gordon, now an established producer, claims to have spent under $15,000 on his *King Dinosaur*—which grossed in excess of $1,000,000.

I borrowed the equipment [he says]. I got friends to act for me, deferred payments, and did the special effects myself. We shot the whole thing in a week at Big Bear. Of course, the locale was supposed to be another planet; but I got around that by having one of the characters say, "Strange! This planet is almost identical to Earth!"

Of course, some films are more ambitious; but the bright young men know that the expense is a negligible item. It's the gimmick that counts.

William Kozlenko, former producer at M-G-M, explains the economic situation this way: "The movie business can be compared, in a sense, to the city of New York. Only very rich or very poor people can live in New York. Only very expensive or very cheap pictures can succeed here."

However, low cost of production is an effect, not a cause: its existence is due wholly to the nature of the demand. And how does one explain the demand?

Arthur L. Mayer was known, some years ago, as Broadway's Merchant of Menace, because of the large number of zombie, mummy and vampire pictures he ran at his Rialto Theatre. He was happy then, because the popularity of his bills seemed to have no significance. Today he is worried. It's strictly young people who support the gruesome-twosomes, he avers, and offers a theory:

The kids are in no mood to enjoy homey little pictures of family life, sweet adolescent love stories, or gallants dueling in doublet and hose. They do not even like brisk, sophisticated comedy with smart dialogue over the martinis. What they want, entertainment-wise, is red meat. If self-identification is the secret of box-office popularity, they find it easier to identify themselves with the sons of Frankenstein, or the granddaughters of Dracula, than with Lindbergh soaring across the Atlantic, or a well-constructed young lady of 20 pursued by a 60-year-old wreck of a once popular leading man.

Mayer regards this absorption in the more repulsive aspects of life as a reflection of the age in which we live. "With justifiable lack of faith in the wisdom of their elders and the competence of their contemporaries, the young people are frustrated, purposeless, bitter." However, even Mr. Mayer, if forced to choose between horror films and the rash of sadistic quickies about juvenile delinquency, would choose horror. The monsters in the latter are less recognizable, he says, and the blood is more likely to be ketchup.

But this seems more a description of the patient's illness than an examination of its causes. "The age in which we live" is a factor, certainly; but only one of many. The others hold surprises, even shocks.

For the first of these, we must make another comparison with Westerns. In both genres, the audience can become directly involved with a clear-cut, understandable situation. The Monster and the Villain are bad, they must be thwarted; the Hero and the Professor (despite his idiosyncrasies) are good, they must triumph; the Heroine and Female Botanist are virtuous, they must be saved. Challenges are to be met, risks to be taken, rewards to be gathered. In both genres, the audience assumes the identity of Nobility saving Virtue from Evil. And there is no shade of gray to spoil the chiaroscuro.

The world today is a confusing place for most of us. The great issues are not clear, as they once were. Bad, we now discover, is not always bad, nor is good invariably good; indeed, bad is quite frequently, under certain conditions, good, and good bad. We cannot hate evil, for evil has become a form of sickness, and it is evil to hate. We are not sure that it is wise to be brave or brave to be wise. Heroes are now corporations, or machines, and villains are countries. The individual is having a hard time. And we can be certain only that we are being undone, doomed, destroyed, or carried on to technological heights of which we never dreamed, by frightening, incomprehensible Forces, and that there is little *we* can do about it.

In this sense, the Modern Age hypothesis is acceptable. Horror films provide up-to-date escape from an overwhelming, always-changing world; they are a panacea to what Edmund Wilson calls "an instinct to inoculate ourselves against panic at the real horrors loose on the Earth." The escape-universe of the Western is positive: it stresses certain questionable virtues and evils and ends on a solidly up-beat note. The world of the science-horror film, in its present form, is negative. It panders to the basic ignorances and prejudices of the motion-picture audience. By suggesting that scientists (i.e., people smarter than thee and me) are untrustworthy lunatics who will kill us all some day with their unholy experiments, it suggests also that science—and progress—are bad. It takes the stand, common in

Pythagoras' time, that too much knowledge is a bad thing and that well enough ought, by God, to be left alone. It even allows the audience to empathize occasionally with the Professor in order to demonstrate how easily one may be led along the road to perdition.

A more profoundly anti-intellectual message could hardly be found than "Curiosity killed the cat," but the horror-film makers have found it. It is:

Curiosity killed the world.

Less complex, but perhaps more accurate, explanations of the phenomenon are supplied by the producers and exhibitors themselves.

"In the first place," says Bert Gordon, "you've got to understand that the movie audience today consists almost entirely of teen-agers. Either they're naive and go to get scared"—this referring to the curious fact that none of the horror films is actually horrible, or terrifying, or remotely scary—"or they're sophisticated and enjoy scoffing at the pictures. There isn't much a teen-ager can scoff at these days, you know."

Accordingly, some enterprising producers have gone to great lengths to make their products corny and unrealistic and "scoffable."

In any case, "Thank God for the horror pictures," says the manager of a large San Fernando, California, Drive-In. "They've saved us. Before this kick we were thinking of shutting down two nights a week; now, with all the monster stuff, the place starts filling up at three o'clock. . . . The kids go for it. The girls yell and hang on to the boys and . . . sometimes you've really got to keep an eye on those cars. . . ."

Which brings us to one of the more startling theories. According to producer Robert Newman, "Horror movies are sexually stimulating to people, whether they know it or not. The monster itself is usually a symbol of sexual power unleashed. . . ."

And there may be something to it. The popular monsters —King Kong, Frankenstein, Dracula, the Creature from the Black Lagoon—are all male, all inveterate skirt-chasers. Though it is never made clear exactly what they plan to do with their quarries, once caught, their intentions are unmistakably dishonorable.

Certain producers in Hollywood sharing this quality in common with the creatures, it is perhaps not surprising that some of them have approached the sex-stimulus angle with the cold-eyed aplomb of TV pollsters.

A careful study of the subject revealed to depth-probers the following information. The appeal of *Dracula* obtains from the Count's habit of sucking blood from the necks of nubile maidens, which in turn suggests perversion. The werewolf continues to enjoy a happy popularity both because he encourages the savage and bestial instinct (with its connotations of human sacrifice, cannibalism, sodomy, and rape) and because, with his sacred ancestry, dating to Zeus Lycaeus, the wolf-god of ancient Greece, he promotes feelings of invulnerability. *The Invisible Man* connotes voyeurism. *The Fifty-Foot Woman* makes possible a sexually literal return to the womb. And so on, to Roger Corman's inventive *Crab Monsters*—which do not call for comment here. At any rate, certain producers decided to be a bit less subliminal about the whole thing, and created a host of frankly phallic monsters. The visitors in *It*

Came from Outer Space left almost nothing to the imagination when they finally appeared, and *The Beast with 1,000,000 Eyes* could not have been more obvious short of Technicolor. Business was sensational.

But the sex theory can be carried too far, as it was in another field, that of automobiles. In each case there is a core of truth, but the hypothesis—so seductive because of the ease of application—tends to become ridiculous after a while. It results in such wildly blatant absurdities as the late Edsel's grille and one independent producer's plan (filched from the Russian composer, Scriabin) to spray essence of musk over his audiences at particularly climactic scenes.

A loftier motive is supplied by psychologists, who feel that people go to the films because "science has robbed them of their religion. Becoming aware of the concept of death, they seek assurance of immortality. The Mad Professors supply that assurance. When a monster is raised from the dead, the audience experiences resurrrection."

From all of which, one would assume that horror movies offer a little of everything to everyone. And the almost inescapable conclusion is that the craze is fast becoming an American institution, a solidly representative part of our culture.

The question of why people go to see the films has been discussed; a far more difficult question remains. Why, in view of the nearly limitless possibilities of the medium, and its generally respectable past, are horror pictures so poor in quality? Horror is, after all, an accepted form of literature. It (again using the term to include such ancillary genres as science-fiction, fantasy, etc.) has been treated by most of history's great authors, including the Apostles. Most of the recognized books for children (Andersen, the brothers Grimm, Baum) deal with horripilatory themes. Stemming as it does from superstition and fear, mankind's deepest emotions, horror can only be regarded as an important subject. There are, literally, hundreds of great horror stories and novels, perhaps a thousand more good ones—all containing the same basic elements as the current creature-features. Yet this literary goldmine has been almost wholly ignored. Why?

To understand the answer, one must first understand the nature of Hollywood, which is impossible. Hollywood is now, and has always been, an unreal place full of unreal people. Like Erewhon or Wonderland, it has its own set of laws, its own set of mores, and these laws and mores are not duplicated anywhere on the face of the earth. Logic is discussed in Hollywood, but the truth is that there is little logic and little thought as it is understood elsewhere in the world. Novelists have tried to describe Hollywood, but the closer they have come to facts, the more they have been accused of embroidering. No such place could exist, the Eastern critics say; and in a sense, the Eastern critics are right. The Hollywood referred to is not so much a place as a form of neurosis. It is simply the movie business and the people connected with it, and that takes in all the territory from Beverly Hills to Palm Springs.

It is not surprising that of all the producers engaged in the business of manufacturing horror films, none will admit to a liking for the subject. Most of them frankly hate it and would vastly prefer to be working on comedies or Westerns or mysteries. "The cycle will pass," said producer Gordon Kaye, hopefully but inaccurately, eight years ago, "and then we'll all celebrate, because it will give us a chance to get back to interesting picture-making."

William Alland is a representative case. He has made several fortunes for himself and his studio on such popular items as *The Creature from the Black Lagoon, The Mole People,* etc. Yet he does not appear to care at all for the medium. As though determined not to suffer alone, he has consistently assigned his pictures to writers who share his sentiments.

Which brings up a widespread misconception. It is thought that the horror films are written by "veteran science-fiction writers," whereas the truth is that these worthies have not had so much as a look in. In any other business it would seem logical to hire a qualified man for a specific job; not so in Hollywood. Alland once allowed Ray Bradbury to confect something called a "treatment" (neither a story nor a screenplay but a mutation of both), but science-fiction's most gifted author was not permitted to touch the actual shooting script. That delicate work was handed to one Harry Essex, a Hollywood pro, who admittedly knew little of *sf*. That the picture (*It Came from Outer Space*) turned out reasonably well is largely due to Essex's faithfulness to the Bradbury original. Most of the really first-rate authors in the field have had to wait by their telephones and watch as hacks and unknowns have picked up the heavy green. Robert Heinlein, referred to by some critics as The Master, has been called upon just twice; Theodore Sturgeon, Isaac Asimov, James Blish, Clifford Simak, the late Henry Kuttner, and Fritz Leiber have not been contacted at all.

There is, of course, no reasonable explanation for this attitude, nor does Hollywood offer any. It can only be concluded therefore that the producers' ignorance of the subject is so profound that they have simply never *heard* of the medium's masters.

This naïveté has, in fact, resulted in a form of illogic hardly credible to the rational mind. The same William Alland, who was in at the start of the craze (kicked off by *Them* and *The Thing,* both interesting pictures), provides numerous examples. When he decided to produce *The Mole People* he hired a man named Laszlo Gorog to write the script. Gorog, whose sole science-fictional qualification consisted of his last name, which is the same spelled backwards, is a Viennese playwright. At the time of his assignment, he had read no science-fiction or horror at all with the exception of a bit of Karel Čapek. He had never heard of Ray Bradbury. The very term "science-fiction" was new to him. Yet he plunged manfully into the job, and though it ended so disastrously that one beleaguered critic called it "the worst film ever made," Alland was apparently delighted, for he forthwith commissioned Gorog to script a monster film called *The Lost Valley.* The Viennese playwright switched to television.

A more adaptable type was Martin Berkeley. He had established a reputation as a Real Pro, having written many of the *Doctor Kildare* and *Lassie* pictures, and therefore seemed the ideal choice for a series of horror films. Immediately upon going under contract, he and Alland began the inevitable Conferences. What sort of horror film should they make? They tried to think of stories, but that got them nowhere. So, feeling that the gimmick was the thing foremost, they trotted down to the Los Angeles County Museum, where they looked at insects and other creatures in amber. Spiders had been used (*Tarantula*), so had ants (*Them*), so had lizards (*King Dinosaur*) but what about—*grasshoppers?* That was it! Berkeley returned to the studio and, after typing out a "formula sheet" based on the successful *Them,* reworked that picture as *The Deadly Mantis.* It made a fortune.

More than that was spent on, and considerably more made by M-G-M's *Forbidden Planet,* which was said to have been thought up one night after a cocktail party by two Hollywood scribes and sold the following morning.

Nothing, on the other hand, resulted from an experiment by Columbia. Someone had told the wazirs that horror was big and that there were actually such stories in existence. Suspiciously, Columbia hired an established science-fiction writer and told him to pick something good. Overcome with excitement, the writer did just that. He picked a lovely yarn by Arthur Machen. It was rejected with a note reading, simply: "Too advanced." Undaunted, the writer picked another yarn, one of the classics. Again, rejected: "Too advanced." He picked another. "Too advanced." He tried stories by Bradbury, M. R. James, Blackwood, de la Mare, Sturgeon, Kuttner—all turned down. Frantic, the writer chose items from *Air Wonder Stories,* on the theory that what was accepted thirty years ago in *sf* circles would not be too advanced in 1958. But the theory was wrong. He ended by writing, while half-loaded, a script called *Killer Brain,* which was about a giant ape with (according to the writer) the brain of a producer. Everyone loved it.

There are hundreds of similar anecdotes, all going to show exactly why the films are as bad as they are. But, in a sense, the situation was unavoidable. For nothing worthwhile ever seems to come out of a commercial craze. The great horror and science-fiction pictures of the past—*King Kong, Frankenstein, Dracula, The Island of Lost Souls, Things to Come, The Man Who Could Work Miracles, Metropolis, The Day the Earth Stood Still, The Body Snatchers, Dead of Night, The Invisible Man, Isle of the Dead, The Cat People, The Cabinet of Doctor Caligari, The Werewolf of London, The Lost World, Just Imagine, Beauty and the Beast, etc., etc.*—were truly independent productions, made for the fun and love of it, mad risks, personal statements of imaginative men. Pains were taken with those pictures, money spent on them, intelligence applied to every foot of film. They had the basic elements of the creature-features we see, or avoid, today: they had monsters and scientists (both mad and sane) and virtuous damsels in deadly peril. But they had something else, those pictures, they had quality. (Even Hammer Films, after a grand start with *The Creeping Unknown* and *X—The Unknown,* has gone the assembly-line route.) It didn't take slavering, foam-flecked, anthropomorphic phalli to chill the blood in those times. All it took was a cold wind slamming an unexpected door, a hand on a banister, the cry of a child, or the silence of a field beneath a moon. But we're in the midst of a craze now and Hollywood can't afford the expense of such effects, because to achieve them you must have a good dramatic story, good dialogue, good direction, good acting, and good photography; and that's where you run into money.

Is there a chance for a return to the horrors of yesteryear? Will the debris and offal and driftwood be swept away by a sudden current of popular good taste?

No one knows for sure, but it seems unlikely. In discussing the horror craze, one unhappy producer put it as well as anyone. "We've created a Monster," he said. "God have mercy on our souls."

Who closed

the castles?

OF THE heavy losses we have sustained, none can be regarded with more melancholy than the loss of the great movie theatres. A mere generation ago, they proliferated. Every city and town had its equivalent of the Roxy, which is to say, its equivalent of the Taj Mahal—or what the Taj Mahal is supposed, by the young, to be. Gigantic palaces they were, those theatres, hung with tapestries and paintings of the stars; with foot-thick crimson carpets, stone fountains in the lobby, exotic plants, no doubt imported from the equatorial jungles, statuary of rare design, costly beyond price, and hundreds of rooms and alcoves to be investigated before ever you entered the vast dark caverns where the movies would be shown. They were the most magnificent, opulent, mysterious, thrilling places in all the world, and the children loved them.

How they operated at a profit, as they did, is difficult to understand. Tickets cost ten cents for kids under twelve (which included everyone under sixteen who knew how to squnch down at the ticket booth, walk normally with his knees bent and assume a childish expression). And thousands more paid nothing, having developed ingenious methods by which they could sneak past the beleaguered management. Of these methods, the two most efficacious were walking in backwards during intermission, and lying ("Honest to God, Mister, I paid, honest, you just ask the lady there, she'll remember."). Of course, the ploys had to be changed as management got wise to them, but they were in endless supply. One could get a friend to open a side exit door, or pass out a stub ("Whattya mean, sneakin' in? Here's the ticket you ripped. Don't'cha remember?"), or divert the usher's attention. Really imaginative kids went to the movies twice a week and did not pay a cent until they were in college.

Also, recall, those were the days of the triple features. If you really enjoyed films, it followed that you sat through the whole bill at least twice, once from the first row, looking straight up at the flickering giants, once from the rear of the highest balcony.

All the great theatres had two or three balconies then. One prowled these levels with one's gang, generally during the draggy sections, or Love Stuff, getting off Good Ones at the top of one's voice. Saturday matinees are still nightmarish to any adults who are imprudent enough to subject themselves voluntarily to the experience, but the edge has been dulled. Children are, on the whole, better behaved today. Where we were infuriating, they are merely annoying.

The utilitarian theatres must be held partially responsible. Somehow they do not seem to invite genuine chaos, in the sense that a cafeteria does not invite leisurely dining. They—

the new or refurbished ones—are too "functional," too clearly what they are: movie theatres. It was not so with the theatres of yesterday. They were palaces, temples, cathedrals, circuses; and the showing of motion pictures seemed nothing more than an added attraction.

Of course they were tasteless in the extreme, mixing styles and periods with cheerful abandon, but they were convincing. Whether the fountain in the lobby was designed by Bellini or by Lob-ee Display, Inc., whether it blended well or badly with the giant mummy case beside it, was of no concern to the kids. The fountain was big and pretty and it had real water in it and that was all that counted.

There was no agreement on the meaning of the word functional then. People would have been likely to ask, Functional for what? Functional to whom? Now it's understood, though not by me, to apply to any unit (house, car, airplane, theatre) shorn of all appurtenances which are not essential to the purpose for which the unit was intended. I would agree to the extent that one should not work bas-reliefs on the exterior of a missile, not for the reason that they are unnecessary, but because they would probably frustrate the missile's purpose. Otherwise I wouldn't mind; it might make a cunning effect.

Anyway, what is the function of a movie theatre? To show films? Yes; but also to enchant children. And what is there in our new theatres to perform this function? What to thrill and excite the young patron and set his skin tingling all the long way to his seat?

What to match Chicago's Woods Theatre in the thirties and forties? In those days, the theatre personnel dressed in costumes corresponding to those worn in the various features.

When the kids flocked to see two complete, joined-together Flash Gordon serials, plus the first chapter of the new one, they paid their money to Dale Arden, handed their ticket to Doctor Zarkov and were shown to their seats by Ming the Merciless. During a long run of *The Mummy,* an exact replica of Karloff's creation limped, arm outstretched, eyes blazing, up and down the block in front of the show, urging everyone to form a single line. Within the lobby one could examine numerous sarcophagi, or ponder ancient papyri, or finger the original Rosetta Stone. And there was a picture, too!

The Woods still stands, as do many of the old palaces of joy. Some of them even show films. But they are sad to behold, and unbearable to visit. For they are temples long since overrun by unbelievers, desecrated, defiled, abandoned. They can only wait. Their fountains dry, their carpets frayed, their balconies empty, they can only wait for the final, inevitable demolition.

A million laughs

THERE IS probably nothing the world wants or needs more today than an epidemic of laughter. Laughter is the great escape valve through which tension and fear and confusion may be released. The world, God knows, is as tense and fearful and confusing as it has ever been. Yet we do not laugh. We chuckle, we snigger, we snicker, we titter, we smile, but we do not laugh; nor have we done so, individually or in concert, for ten long solemn years. "We" being everybody, of course, but Americans in particular. Mirth was one of our principal products not so long ago. We exported it in gross quantities to the four corners of the earth, creating thereby an image of the United States as the capital of joy and merriment, a happy-go-lucky, fun-loving nation of clowns who preferred pie in the face to pie in the sky, exploding cigars to imploding bombs, and the boff to and above all things.

It was not a very dignified image, to be sure. But, curiously enough, America's prestige was at its peak in those days, whereas now that we take ourselves seriously, as the hard-hitting, no-nonsense Leaders of the Free World, our prestige has plummeted almost to the vanishing point. People used to like us. They might disagree with us and even fight us, sometimes, but always—even from our worst enemies—there was the admission (however grudging) of an abiding fondness and respect for the Yanks. Now we are among the least liked and least respected of countries, scorned, vilified, resented, ridiculed. And, whether or not there is a connection, it all started when we forgot how to laugh.

Laughter is the sound a nation makes when it is proud of its past and confident of its future. We made that sound, and amplified it to decibels unreached before or since, for the forty glorious years between 1910 and 1950 that marked the era of screen comedy.

As usual, we didn't invent the form, nor were we its sole practitioners; but we were responsible for its development into an art and for most of its greatest moments. Until the advent of "talkies" we were universally accepted as the absolute and supreme creators of film humor, not only without peers but also without serious competition. And no wonder. We had the best directors, the best gag men, the best comics and no less than three authentic geniuses.

The geniuses are gone: dead, retired, or in exile. So are the comics. It is generally thought that their breed is proliferating, but that is incorrect. The men we call comics today—Mort Sahl, Lenny Bruce, Shelley Berman, Jonathan Winters, Bob Newhart, et al.—are highly skilled entertainers; but they are in no sense comics, for the response they seek from their audiences is not laughter but understanding. And while it is true that they do manage to fetch an occasional guffaw, it is also true that not a single one of these clever, caustic, cynical, disillusioned young men could have got himself hired as assistant gatekeeper when comedy was in flower. No value judgment is involved. Stand-up comedians are neither better nor worse than true comics; they are simply different, as an ichthyologist, say, is different from a fisherman. They are all well-groomed, respectable—if slightly harassed—looking fellows. During the course of their acts they move perhaps a total of three feet in any direction, slowly. They use neither props nor costumes, if one discounts Mort Sahl's rolled-up newspaper and sloppy sweater, which one does. Their appeal is to the head, via the ears, and for that reason they are enormously popular with people who know them only through their record albums.

The true comic, of course, must be seen to be disbelieved. Unreal, insubstantial as a shadow, apart from humanity and above its petty course, he thrives—as did the first comic and god of all joy, Pan—in the country of dreams, which is an international, inter-racial, interdenominational and wholly nonexclusive community. No surprise, then, that he throve as never before or since in the age of the silent motion picture. In his new incarnation he chased across the world, kicking down barriers en route, breaking into the private heart of every mere human who saw him; and it is our pride that he made his home America.

Look at him now; forget the present and look at him: Pan's great-great-great-grandchild thrice removed, Tartar-mustached, uniformed, helmeted, seated high on the bucking back of a car that never existed, in a world that never was, pell-mell on his way to glory. See how he wrestles manfully with the wheel

and keeps his eyes on the road, to no avail: the ridiculous
Squad Car caroms from curb to curb like a thing possessed,
smashing store fronts, uprooting hydrants, leveling the population. The fact that those attentive eyes are crossed in a manner
unknown to ophthalmology would seem to pertain to the vehicle's erratic flight, but remember, this is the world of comedy,
where only the abnormal is normal. Look at the car itself.
Surely no control is possible over a machine whose components
have scarcely a nodding acquaintance one with the other. The
wheels, disdainful of their axles, wobble and pivot frantically,
causing the fenders to flap in a desperate effort to leave the
body. The windshield, already reduced to a glassless frame,
flies off, taking with it the helmet of another of Pan's descendants. Turning to follow the course of his headpiece, the
divine Cop fails to observe a low-hanging tree branch which
is approaching fast. *Pow!* It sweeps the Cop aloft and deposits
him in the midst of a vegetable pushcart, staffed by a volatile
Italian who promptly whips a stiletto from beneath his apron
and pursues the luckless victim up a nearby alley.

Now back to the Squad Car, which still contains a gigantic
overload of Cops. Watch as it careens around a sharp turn,
mounts the curbing, runs a few yards along the sidewalk,
scrapes some of its cargo off onto a striped awning and plunges
back into a maelstrom of traffic—headed the wrong way on a
one-way street.

The inevitability of disaster! Gesticulating wildly, the Cops
clang their alarm bell and weave through the onrushing cas-
cade of automobiles, miraculously avoiding collision after collision as they hurry to the scene of some imaginary crime. In a
breathless moment the vehicle spins crazily around another

corner and leaps like a frolicsome colt toward a railroad grade crossing, where it coughs, shivers and stops, in the exact center of the track.

And here comes the Limited, black smoke boiling from its stubby stack, white steam hissing from its sides. Catastrophe! The Cops are trying frantically to restart the balky car. Their cross-eyed Chief hops up and down, urging them on. It is no use. Do they push the doomed vehicle out of harm's way? Of course not! The Chief and his men rush down the tracks *to-ward* the oncoming juggernaut, their arms outthrust in a magnificent gesture of defiance.

But the train is not impressed. Chuffing and puffing madly, it bears down upon the clutch of Cops. Five yards; four yards; three; two . . . At the last possible instant the hapless hooligans come to their senses, tumble headlong out of the thundering bolide's path, down an embankment, *splash!* into a muddy ditch—just as the crazy Squad Car shakes itself to life and roars away, missing annihilation by inches.

Now, separated from their conveyance by the speeding train, the frustrated minions of the law stand mired in the muck until the track is cleared. Then, hopelessly but bravely, they start a mad, wonderful chase after the driverless car, disappearing into the distance and fading into the end title of a Keystone comedy.

Neither the alpha nor the omega of screen comedy, the Keystone Cops have come to symbolize the form, as the picture of a quiet, Ivy League-suited young man standing on a concert stage may be said to symbolize current American humor. The Cops flashed across comedy's horizon as a kind of cosmic afterthought in the creation of film pantomime. Yet, though they disappeared like any bright meteorite, their principal activities—violent, almost mayhemic assault; perpetration of lese majesty on any figure of dignity; and the chase, invariably devastating, inevitably catastrophic—were an encapsulation of the format. Other, individual talents brought wry, sardonic, satirical or pathetic refinements, but the Cops and their madcap machinations remain as spokesmen for the period.

What is little known, even to those who are rediscovering movie comedy's great past through such television programs as *Silents, Please,* is the fact that certain films were drawing hysterical laughter almost two full decades before Sennett's gaggle of uniformed dolts ever mounted the back step of their tired Model T. The first of these—and the first of all time—derived its effect from a simple function of nature: the sneeze.

Although not designed as a comic masterpiece, the dignity-destroying film clip shot at Thomas A. Edison's studio (The Black Maria) in 1893 rates as the granddaddy Adam. The brief episode did no more than to record Fred Ott, one of Edison's employees, in the process of launching an involuntary oronasal blast. It would have remained in obscurity with hundreds of other minute reels made for the company's peep-show Kinetoscope had not the transition from these one-viewer-at-a-time machines to projected exhibition been made shortly thereafter. The explosive snort, albeit without the benefit of sound, afforded a change of pace for audiences already beginning to tire of shots of breaking surf, waterfalls, trains in motion and dancers, "all wonderfully real and singularly exhilarating." *The Sneeze* brought howls of laughter, and film humor was begun.

The first comedy with a "plot" followed soon afterward when the Lumiére brothers produced an interlude entitled

Teasing the Gardener. It was simple-minded and primitive but, for the times, nothing short of an epic. The scene is a garden, somewhere in France. A tousle-haired little girl skips gaily among the flowers until she encounters a hose. She gazes at it for a long moment, then, giggling, jumps upon it with both feet, shutting off the water supply. As the surprised gardener peers at the nozzle, the little girl steps off the hose—with results that kept audiences in stitches all around the world.

The names of the principals in this first film comedy team have been lost to posterity, but the splosh of liquid full in the unsuspecting face introduced a "turn" to be followed devoutly by hundreds of comics in thousands of reels to come.

Another sequence filmed the same year, similar to *Teasing the Gardener* but containing somewhat more depth of characterization and heaviness of plot, was Robert W. Paul's *The Soldier's Courtship*. In this one a uniformed young man and a nursemaid are shown in the act of pitching enthusiastic but discreet woo. They are on a park bench. An old lady appears. She sits down on the bench. For obscure reasons she begins to edge close to the idyllic couple. Annoyed, the soldier and his girl stand up, abruptly. The seat tips, the old lady is dumped to the ground, and the bench tumbles on top of her. THE END.

It sounds cruel, but it was not, for the old lady wasn't real except insofar as she *represented* reality. As with all film humor to follow, the action of *The Soldier's Courtship* took place in a world of its own making. The same scene encountered in the real world would have embarrassed and appalled all those who laughed so freely. (Buster Keaton proves this whenever he goes through one of his famous and hilarious screen routines for TV's *Candid Camera*. Most people, unaware of his identity and oblivious to the fact that they are watching a great comedian at work, react out of profound discomfort. No one ever seems to be genuinely amused.)

Londoner Paul realized that he had found a good thing and went on to establish the first comedy film studio. By 1903 the pattern of the comical short subject was fixed. It became a known quantity. John Montgomery relates of these pioneer epics in his *Comedy Films* that:

. . . a man would be seen running wild—perhaps in a nightshirt— dashing downhill on roller skates, through barrels and past dray carts and cabs, miraculously avoiding danger, while the audience gasped a series of "Oooohhs!," knowing full well that soon he would finish up in the lake, or in a bin of flour, oil, soot, molasses, paint, glue, dough or treacle. As the film was no respecter of old age or dignity, audiences soon became used to the hilarious spectacle of the infirm, the blind, the rich and the poor (but more especially the rich and haughty), the parson and the policeman—all being caught out in ridiculous circumstances. Mothers-in-law now found themselves not only on the stage, but also on the screen. Elderly gentlemen with ear trumpets now became the object of ribald mirth, for could not all the flour, oil, soot, molasses, etc., be poured down the ear trumpet? The misfortunes of others were from the first infant flickerings a cue for hearty laughter, as absurdity was piled on top of absurdity. Meanwhile the hazards of the chase included animals, the lame and the halt, the drunk and the sober, the pursued and the pursuer. The heroine's gouty uncle, chasing the hero, would receive little sympathy either in the film or from the audience. He would most certainly end up with his gouty foot firmly stamped on and his niece stolen from him; and he could consider himself lucky to escape the dreaded flour, oil, soot, molasses, and other devilish ingredients of the average comedy.

This apparently brutal method of euchring forth audience reaction stemmed, of course, from the similar efforts of a legion of stage comics who had been belting each other with inflated pigs' bladders and pairs of bed slats (the original "slapstick") for a century or more. The latitude of film technique, however, gave not only freedom of movement but virtually free rein to the use of props which could not be employed on the reasonably tidy stage. Thus stage and screen comedy methods were divorced forever.

Actually, few of the established legitimate clowns of the time ever attempted the transition to celluloid. The big names, who had sharpened their acts over a long period of years, could not countenance "posing for the flickers" and displaying their talents in exchange for the few paltry dollars a week offered by the early producers. Nor were they able to grasp the notion, put forward by Paul, that these same dollars would be adequate recompense for devising altogether new routines—routines which, if properly spread out, could carry a good act through a lifetime of vaudeville dates. So the way was cleared for Keaton, Chaplin, Arbuckle, Turpin, Langdon, Lloyd and other unknowns to grasp fate by the scruff of its baggy pants and wrest from it fame and fortune.

The millions to be poured into the industry and transferred to selected bank accounts were not even suspected when America's first film comedy star waddled before the cameras, in 1910. A portly, legitimate actor who longed to play romantic leads, John Bunny mastered the art of pantomime because he had been told that this accomplishment, added to his hippopotamic bulk, would make him an ideal clown. Good natured, pliable, and quite talented, Bunny brought a Dickensian sort

of character to the miniscule Vitagraph motion-picture company in Brooklyn and soon the characterization catapulted
him to world renown. At that time, the movies had already
swept around the globe in a kind of entertainment tidal wave.
People loved pictures of all kinds, but especially Bunny's. His
half-sad, half-ridiculous face, Micawber's if it was anyone's,
smiled out of 150 one- and two-reelers and brought untold joy
to the land.

Less concerned with joy and more devoted to assault with
intent to commit great bodily harm were Al Christie and Mack
Sennett, a couple of embryonic tycoons who managed to develop an almost magical rapport with the audiences of the day.
Sennett, the discoverer, employer and mentor of all the slapstick stars except Keaton and Lloyd, was unquestionably a
genius—to everyone but himself. He never laid claim to the
sobriquet nor to any particular skills other than an inherent
sense of the ridiculous and the conviction that whatever made
him laugh was bound to make the average man laugh, too.
Yet, though Christie's productions occasionally rivaled Sennett's, the Keystone fun factory must be evaluated as the single
greatest source of motion-picture amusement ever in operation,
thanks primarily to the screwball vision of its proprietor.

A stage-struck expatriate Canadian steelworker, Mack Sennett was playing the rear end of a two-man comic horse when
movie fame beckoned. The gesture arrived in the form of an
invitation to act before the camera of D. W. Griffith, a director
of small but growing reputation. Sennett leaped at the opportunity, but it was no bold step calculated to cut him off
from the legitimate stage. It was simply a temporary answer
to a permanent problem: poverty. Inasmuch as he was almost

chronically unemployed and subsisting on free-lunch-counter snacks at the time, he was in no position to turn down any job, however remote its connection with show business.

Such early experiences with penury may fairly be said to have made Sennett the colorful and contradictory figure he became. Where money and monetary values were concerned he was hopelessly inconsistent. He would think nothing of paying thousands of dollars a week to writers who never wrote, or of firing bricklayers who fell a half-dozen short of the daily quota of bricks. He would build a tower from which to spy on the entire company and then, the next week, outfit and staff an entire studio for a star who would not even let him inside the gate. These traits, and a host of similar idiosyncrasies —plus his fantastic record of producing over *one thousand* hit films—make the King of Comedy one of the most enchanting figures of this shadowy domain.

He worked hard for Griffith in the beginning, but could never develop much fondness for the great man. "[He] was kind to me," Sennett reported some years later, "but his kindness was something like the generosity of an emperor who gives away continents. He made his pronouncements as if he were handing the Ten Commandments to Moses. He was exactly my own age."

The relationship lasted only a short time, but Sennett later credited his absorption of the Griffith innovations for his own ability to polish the rough stone of slapstick into a more valuable bauble.

In 1912, when Mack persuaded two bookmakers, Charlie Bauman and Adam Kessel, to refrain from tearing his head off in lieu of payment for a hundred-dollar bad guess on the relative speed of a group of thoroughbreds—and, indeed, to further extend him $2500 to form Keystone Productions— there were in existence seven accepted types of comedies. Foremost was the Chase; then came the Trick Photographic Film, the Knockabout, the Dramatic Farce, the Domestic or Social Comedy, the Satirical Comedy, and the Cartoon Film. Sennett was to lump all these categories together in as many combinations as possible in each and every epic, thus creating a new art.

Rule Number One of the art demanded that life's portrait be painted with a brush a yard wide on the end of a ten-foot handle. However, contrary to popular belief, Keystone's King never had a wild, everything-goes philosophy. He insisted that his superficially chaotic burlesques proceed from believable premises. For example: It is believable that an attractive cook should work in a mansion and that others should covet the job. It is therefore no strain on the credibility to show a jealous rival inserting a stick of dynamite in a rising loaf of bread being prepared by the cook, or flooding the kitchen, or pouring hot pepper into the soup. Motivation was the key to Keystone. The clowns could do anything that came into their heads so long as they were properly, or even improperly, motivated.

Parody was also big at the fun factory. To Sennett, conventional stage plays and motion pictures (particularly of the heavily dramatic variety) were only fodder for the grist mill, to be chewed into instantly recognizable bits and spewed out like cornflakes. In keeping with the concept that comedy is the satire of tragedy, the more serious and complex the original work, the more ridiculous and simple-minded the parody. Such titles as *The Sea Squawk, Uncle Tom Without a Cabin,*

East Lynne with Variations and *The Battle of Who Run* suggest typical irreverence. *Tillie's Punctured Romance,* the first full-length feature comedy and the vehicle which established Marie Dressler as a comedienne of the highest rank, did much to propel Charlie Chaplin, Mack Swain, Edgar Kennedy, Charlie Chase and Mabel Normand along the road to fame. It was merely a take-off on Miss Dressler's highly successful stage play, *Tillie's Nightmare,* in which she had introduced the grand old tear-jerking ballad, *Heaven Will Protect the Working Girl.*

The story of how this howler came to be is typical of the methods by which movies were made in the Golden Age. Sennett was determined to produce a feature-length comedy. Everyone advised him against it. He refused to listen. He hammered and badgered and hectored his partners Bauman and Kessel, the ex-bookies, until—with grave misgivings— they agreed to ante up $200,000 for the production. Of course, Sennett had no script. He had no ideas. In fact, he now had nothing but two hundred grand and a vague determination to launch Marie Dressler as a Keystone star. He hired the actress at the then fantastic salary of $2500 a week; then he ordered his "scenario department" to create a suitable piece.

The thought of sustaining a chase through six reels was a powerful narcotic for the "writers." They attacked the problem with gusto but, after a week, pronounced it a hopeless and impossible proposition. Sennett was undisturbed. Calling his two top-bracket gagmen into a hotel room in downtown Los Angeles, the King had a case of iced champagne delivered, then locked the door, putting the key in his vest pocket.

"Have all the champagne you want, boys," he said, good-naturedly. "We don't leave this room until we get a story for Marie Dressler."

Thus inspired, and with three bottles still to go, Craig Hutchinson, the senior member of the team, came up with the money-saving idea of using the story line of Miss Dressler's stage hit.

It was a fairly complex piece of dramaturgy in the original, but the Keystone boys soon reduced it to its essentials. Charlie Chaplin played the heavy, a slicker working the farm-country rubes. He meets Tillie (Marie Dressler) and persuades her to steal her father's money and run away with him. In the city they encounter Charlie's ex-mistress and partner-in-crime, Mabel Normand, and soon she has the little operator in her clutches again. Mabel and Charlie get Marie drunk, Charlie steals the money-laden purse and he and his inamorata flee. Shortly, Marie's rich uncle is reported dead and she becomes a wealthy heiress. Charlie returns, sweeps her off her feet again and marries her. They buy a huge home and decide to warm it with a fancy blow-out. In the midst of this the rich uncle, whose death report was greatly exaggerated, arrives. (Remember: this is the simplified version.) Follows then a full-fledged chase involving all the Keystone Cops and innumerable hazards. Charlie is finally taken into custody as the two girls, bound in friendship now by their mutual disaffection for the little conniver, exchange congratulations.

Around that absurd and tangled plot the Sennett gagmen and actors wove a rich tapestry of humor that has kept the film in circulation for forty-six years, solely on its merits as a laugh-getter. Issued at the same time as D. W. Griffith's *Birth of a Nation, Tillie* can be shown for sheer entertainment, while

the Griffith masterpiece is primarily of historical interest. That
it was the great trail-blazer and a work of creative genius is
undeniable; but only the fanatically faithful could argue that
it has not dated to the point of quaintness. *Tillie,* of course,
was quaint to begin with.

As was Sennett, also to begin with. Always money-con-
scious, he was one of the early sun-seekers who flocked to California on the excuse of less rain, more production. In pressuring
Bauman and Kessel into the move, he rashly promised that he
would have a completed comedy in the can within a week after
landing in Los Angeles. Taking Mabel Normand, Ford Sterling, Fred Mace and a cameraman named Pathé Lerhman with
him, Sennett debarked from the cross-country train ride and
walked right into a Shriner's parade. The street was clogged.
Passage was impossible. To a lesser man, this would have been
an inconvenience; to the Comedy King it was a blessing.

Quickly estimating the dramatic possibilities apart from
straight crowd material, the newly arrived director-producer
dispatched his minions in all directions, instructing them to
return with suitable props: a doll, a shawl, an overcoat, and
anything else they might think of. Meanwhile he and Lehrman
set up the tripod. Within minutes, the cast reassembled. Patheti-
cally attired in a shawl and clutching a most realistic baby doll,
Mabel Normand flung herself into the parade under orders to
"embarrass those Shriners! . . . Make out that you are a poor,
lorn working girl, betrayed in the big city, searching for the
father of your child!"

[She] put on the comicalest act you ever clapped eyes on [Mack
reported later], pleading, stumbling, holding out her baby—and the
reactions of those good and pious gentlemen in the parade were

something you couldn't get in six days of D. W. Griffith rehearsals. Men were horrified, abashed, dismayed. One kind soul dropped out and tried to help Mabel.

"Move in, Ford!" I told Sterling. Ford leaped in and started a screaming argument with the innocent Shriner who didn't know he was being photographed to make a buck for Keystone. The police moved in on Ford and Mabel. Ford fled, leaping, insulting the police and they—God bless the police!—they chased him. I helped the cameraman and we got it all. The Shriners were good but the best scenes we nabbed were the running cops. I never got their names but if there are any retired members of the Los Angeles Police Department who remember taking part in that incident, let them bask in fame: They were the original Keystone Cops.

Mabel made out magnificently.

Sennett and his menagerie didn't even stop at their hotel but went directly to a previously rented studio. There they shot enough additional footage to give some sense to the parade scene and had their first one-reeler in the can, not in the promised week, but in a day—thus establishing a Keystone tradition for taking advantage of every possible free action. Whenever a building was to be wrecked, a smokestack toppled, an auto, bicycle, or foot race staged, a channel swim promoted, or an Iowa picnic eaten, Keystone cameramen were on hand. A bakery worker's strike provided the basic ingredient for one film, several fires near the studio resulted in a rash of Firemen comedies, and when the Los Angeles Water Department drained the lake in a downtown park, Sennett had his principals gathered for the greatest mud sequence ever captured on celluloid. Mack also maintained a close friendship with Thomas H. Ince, an early tycoon who often had a veritable army of extras on twenty-four hour call. On such occasions Ince would telephone Sennett and say, "I've got a thousand Indians sitting on their butts. Can you use them?" Keystone would rally a feature player or two and come up with a comedy of the plains.

In his first year of operation in the studio at Edendale, a long-since absorbed suburb of Los Angeles, Sennett issued one hundred and forty comedies. These one- and two-reelers cost about $25,000 each and returned $75,000 to $80,000 in the 1914–1918 period. Humor was a vital part of the motion-picture business then, so the only limits to Keystone's fortunes were the limits of time and inspiration.

The inspiration was largely in the fertile minds of the comics themselves. "Writers" abounded at Keystone and were treated with great respect, even being permitted their own secluded domain; but for many years they were forbidden to go near pen, pencil, paper, or typewriter—on threat of instant dismissal. Their job was to dream up story lines and supplementary bits. They needed nimble minds and India-rubber bodies, for, as noted, they never actually *wrote* (male secretaries were considered adequate to that secondary task) but, instead, *pitched* their brainstorms, usually in the presence of Sennett, his clowns and his directors. With as many as six hardy scriveners writhing and pratfalling to illustrate their gags, it is not surprising that insanity lurked near the surface in every two-reel skein of celluloid.

Yet those early screen writers did not complain, and on the whole it may be observed that theirs was a better and more rewarding life than that endured by most of the current membership of the Writers Guild of America. Despite the apparent indignity of their position, the Edendale gagmen enjoyed unique prestige; also, this "miscellany of wags, bonded together by the loose camaraderie of contempt" liked each other. Nowhere could a happier, or zanier, group of employees be found. However, they did reserve one objection. It was in the area of diet.

The Keystone lot was the first to maintain its own cafeteria. It was well stocked with provender, but the waitresses were strictly forbidden to serve the scenario staff anything more nourishing than a tuna sandwich and a glass of milk during luncheon. "Eating heavy stuff makes them logy," said Sennett, "and they go to sleep, or if they don't go to sleep they get dopey and don't know what they are talking about." To further discourage noontime food intake, the King located his lunchroom at the top of four flights of stairs, of which every fourth step was missing entirely. To prevent scurvy and malnutrition in his literary hirelings, he served "tea" in the afternoon. This tiffin was originally scheduled at four o'clock in the Boss's office but gradually it extended until, at last, long shadows from the nearby hills were cloaking the stages in darkness at teatime. Concluding the repast, Sennett would announce: "Well, boys, now that we've eaten, we can do some more work"—and the loving crew would be kept busy until nine P.M. and beyond.

The Boss was also a demanding taskmaster when it came to his product. He exercised two kinds of quality control: on hearing the "story" and on seeing the finished print. "He could be persuaded to try anything, once," reports an ex-Keystone gagster, "but if he didn't laugh when he saw it on the screen, look out!"

In the coffin-like projection room, there were three rustic benches, such as might be found in a backwoods church. Mack had a large rocking chair for himself and sat, one leg tucked under him, like a half-Buddha. He clasped his hands over his belly and analyzed his product. When a gag failed to make Mack laugh, the men automatically deleted or re-shot that piece of business. If he did laugh, they made a note of that too, for if Mack Sennett laughed, they knew that ten million Americans would howl. His taste was the most infallible audience barometer in the history of motion picture burlesque. He *never* missed.

Gene Fowler described the process of judgment.

Fowler, faithful chronicler of the lives of Hollywood's gamier and more succulent denizens, goes on to an interesting personal character evaluation of the King of Comedy, whom he cherished.

Beneath the odd and fantastic didoes of this brooding keeper of the clowns and despite his suspicious moods, his penchant for baths, for champagne with corned beef and raw onions, the truncated Panama hat and his ponderous but intense love for Mabel Normand, his literary shortcomings and educational poverty, his liberality with temperamental people on the one hand and unyielding taskmasterlike behavior on the other—beneath these evidences of muddled majesty, one feels rather than sees evidences of a compelling simplicity of purpose, a tenacious, strong, driving power that made him the Napoleon of the cap and bells. In his almost primitive soul there existed the average man's instinctive dread of destiny and innate yearning for revolt. He created for himself and for the millions of the earth a voodoo heaven of violent laughter. He provided a means of emotional escape as raucous as a prison-break. . . . His High Priests of pantomime caricatured earth's hourly problems, injustices and defeats in a manner that seemed peculiarly real in the midst of the unreality. . . . The tyrannies of smug dignity fell beneath Sennett's slapstick blows.

Perhaps he had the greatest sense of the ridiculous of any man of modern times.

The Keystone Cops are fixed, chasing through the consciousness of every movie-goer, including those who never saw them. We know *Tillie's Punctured Romance*. But what of the rest of the madness? What, actually, was the flickering, two-dimensional idiocy spawned by this legendary Custard College Dean over the years? Idiot dust now, most of it. Flashes of memory. Bits and pieces. Yet the human mind is a great even-temperature preserver; legends keep forever in its dark vaults. The plots of those revered frolics, hilarious in retrospect, are far too frail to afford any amusement or insight in the telling. They powder away under analysis. But a look at the performers, their work and the social climate in which they operated provides an utterly revealing, and almost tactile, picture of that phenomenal time.

Like Kepler's astronomical Law of Three Bodies, the interaction of these conditions—the almost unbelievable awards of wealth and public acclaim possible, the consequent pressure to improve each performance over the foregoing, and the fluid nature of the medium itself—brought to fruition certain almost predictable denouements. Just to work at the Keystone lot (reverently referred to by employees and rivals alike as "The Pig Sty") was exhilarating, exciting, nerve-racking, and not a little hazardous. Rambling over twenty-eight acres of desertlike hillside, the Edendale studio presented an air of hopeless confusion. Dominating the scene was Sennett's spy-tower, which was in turn dominated by a monumental bathtub, eight feet long, hewn from marble and surmounted by silver fixtures. Sennett,

a passionate bather, did his best thinking in a watery environment, so most of his business dealings were conducted over the
splash of suds (kept high and bright by Abdullah, a former
wrestler turned bathroom attendant and chief masseur). Legend
has it that gagmen were often invited into the tub if they
pleased their Maharaja, but whether there was community
bathing in the two-ton *objet d'art* is not recorded.

In any case, it is unlikely. Sennett, almost prudish about sex
in his comedies or on the lot, hired police matrons to chaperone
his famous Bathing Beauties, and forbade employment to
women who might have entry to the necessarily dark labs or
cutting rooms. Off the premises, however, was something else
again. The King fully realized the inevitable laws of nature
and their side effects. One fabulous episode even found him
taking the entire working force to Mexico in order to confound
a teen-aged starlet who, for various reasons, was preparing to
level a statutory rape charge. Sennett himself was not involved,
but the voluptuous minx had been so familiarly known by so
many employees that the blow might fall anywhere. Tipped
off by a call from a friendly district attorney, Sennett moved
with characteristic swiftness, running up and down the lot,
kicking at dressing-room doors, like a horseless Paul Revere.
"Get your things, we've got to leave the country!" cried the
King of Comedy. *"Everybody!"*

Among those summoned forth by the blast were Mabel
Normand and Polly Moran. After listening to the reason for
the sudden move, Mabel asked in amazement: "You don't
think the D.A. suspects *us,* do you?"

The distraught Sennett barely paused in his flight to spread the alarm. "Everybody's guilty until proved innocent, that's the law. Hurry up!"

The Mexican idyll was not a vacation with pay, the company soon discovered. Sombreros, embroidered vests and roses-in-the-teeth *señoritas* merely replaced baggy pants and nurse-maids for a while.

In such soil, how could creativity fail to flourish?

Explosions of all kinds, including the literal, were the rule at Keystone. Invariably a writer or director, stuck for a smash ending, would contrive to insert a stick of dynamite into the action. In one blast, slightly miscalculated for strength, a giant water tank was ruptured and the studio deluged with tons of water. So inured were the comics and technicians that, instead of retreating in panic, they either worked the flood into whatever they happened to be shooting or shot around it until the stages dried out. Such an occurrence today, of course, would result in loss of production time and a fat insurance claim; but so wonderfully tenuous were the "scripts" for these dramatic *mésalliances* that *any* accident could be worked into the action.

The accident, the gag, the ghastly occurrence, the improbable sequel were flesh, blood and soul of the short comedy. No time was ever wasted developing character or building a message. The hero, heroine, heavy and innocent bystander were instantly recognizable. They were hurriedly but well motivated and put through their tricks. Yet there was mathematical method to the apparent madness.

For example: Sennett stipulated that every gag must be started, pointed and consummated in twenty feet of film. By fiat the reverberation of each explosive charge must be quivering on the air as another was fused. The King achieved many of these effects by means of cutting, frequently to the point of real vivisection: he would think nothing of "trimming" a production by fifty percent. So much fat was chopped from some Keystone frolics that educational subjects, on the canning of tuna fish or the weaving of baskets, were tacked on just to fill out the reels. These innocuous, and wholly incongruous, bits were not unwelcome: they afforded theatre patrons a chance to get their breath and wipe tears of laughter from their eyes without missing anything of importance.

The necessity for meshing hazardous stunts or gags smoothly into the finished product was underlined by Buster Keaton, whose approach to comedy was similar to Sennett's even though the two geniuses never worked together. He says that one of the funniest sight gags he ever devised had to be eliminated from his early masterpiece, *The Navigator,* purely for reasons of bad counterpoint. In the picture, Keaton is alone on a beached ship, near a cannibal-infested island.

To save her [the craft] and myself [he tells], I went underwater in a diver's outfit in a heroic effort to dislodge the ship. I set up a sawhorse labeled "Men at Work" in the sand at the bottom of the sea; I caught a swordfish and when another swordfish attacked me I used the first fish to duel with him; when I got my hands dirty while at the bottom of the sea I washed them in a bucket of water. Finding I had forgotten my pliers, I picked up a lobster which bit a wire in two with his claws. The gag that failed was my favorite and it cost a lot of money. I had the property department construct 1,200 rubber fish, each about fourteen inches long. These were suspended on strings that the audience couldn't see. We used a big machine that looked like a printing press to revolve them in front of the camera. The effect we got was that of a large school of fish passing by in a steady stream. One big fish came up but could not get through the school. To solve his problem I pick up a starfish that is clinging to a rock, attach it to my chest and start directing the piscatorial traffic like a submarine traffic cop. The stream of fish passing by stops, the big fellow crosses, then I wave the school to go on.

The gag, which caused audiences to howl when shown in a Coming Attraction trailer, fell completely dead during several preview showings and had to be deleted. The decision was reached after a conference by the comedy group, whose members rationalized that the action was not one which the diver, hard at work to save himself and his girl, would take time for in the press of the moment. Even though the sequence was a spoof, there was throughout the picture—as throughout every good comedy, however wacky—a slender but strong thread of logic, which could be stretched but not broken.

Those who recognized this basic fact, who understood the necessity for a connection with the vital world, prospered; those who did not bother to provide a string for their pearls perished. Chaplin, Ben Turpin, Fatty Arbuckle and many others emerging from the anonymity of "the gang" used the device—which we may call the device of art—to establish a rapport with the audience that flashes magically from the screen after the passage of nearly half a century.

The great clowns insured a measure of audience sympathy by creating a world populated mainly by scamps, scoundrels, shysters, outcasts and fakes (for all of whom there is secret admiration in every heart), with pretty girls to be loved, and policemen to be eluded. "The successful, well groomed, alert and smart American never appears," as Gilbert Seldes once commented. Actually, it would have been a thespian labor for the majority of Sennett's comics to create the role of a well-groomed, alert, smart American: hardly any of them—or the other reigning pantomime artists—had been afforded the opportunity to rise to the so-called norm until their success as comedians permitted the pose. Chaplin had been a London slum waif and, in that period, still lived as though he expected poverty to be his permanent companion; Roscoe Arbuckle had been a steamfitter and roustabout between scarce vaudeville jobs before bringing his bulk to the attention of Mack Sennett; Ben Turpin, eyes crossed by an accident that made him a fortune, had been a totally undistinguished and underpaid vaudevillean; Keaton, who spent exactly one day in school, had led the abnormal life of a child born in a theatre trunk; W. C. Fields had run away from home and spent his formative years on the bum. It would have been surprising—and probably wholly unamusing—to find anything of the "normal American" in a character brought to life by one of these flour-faced artisans. Yet in their parody of reality, they frequently came closer to human truth than their "straight" competitors. Which, after all, is the normal American—Charlie's Tramp or John Boles's well-groomed, alert, smart young man?

The first of the individuals to poke his head above the bubbling mass of wrestlers, cops, old women, flea-circus entrepreneurs, acrobats, jugglers, prize fighters, dogs, lions, geese and chimpanzees that populated Sennett's Edendale plant—and the first to demand billing plus a sizable increase in salary—was Ford Sterling, for years the "Chief" of the Keystone Cops. Sterling had created a "Dutch" comic in vaudeville and continued it in the Keystone flickers, but it was his inspired direction of his uniformed subordinates during their continual exigencies that won him public acclaim and placed him above specialists like Hank Mann and Chester Conklin. Sennett, unwilling to part with his friend and cohort, upped the comic's salary to $250 per week when $125 was tops. However, the inevitable interview came. Sterling announced that he was quitting. Sennett went to $400. Sterling demurred. The King named $750, with no options in the contract. Sterling leaped like a ballet dancer and threw his hat in the air. "Yippee! So that's what I'm worth!" he crowed. Sennett replied that what he was worth and what he was being offered were not necessarily the same thing, but that anyway it was nice to know that the Chief would stay. "Stay, hell!" Sterling roared. "I'm still leaving. I just wanted to find out what I can get somewhere else."

The star's departure (into eventual obscurity) left Sennett looking for a lead comic.

Chaplin was found and offered $75.00 per week on a year's contract. His salary from Karno's operation was then $50 per week. The offer was, therefore, quite tempting; yet it smelled of danger and risk, so Chaplin refused—or thought he did. If a demand for triple the amount offered wasn't a refusal, then what was it? Sound business instinct, as it turned out. Sennett agreed.

Chaplin, who had never until now known security, was still inclined to stick with Karno; but fellow trouper Alf Reeves talked him out of that. After much indecision, he signed the contract.

Working with veterans like Arbuckle, Mack Swain, Charley

Chase, Slim Summerville, Hank Mann and Al St. John at the fevered pace of the Keystone one-reelers almost caused the timid, shy little comic to vanish. His first film, *Making a Living,* was highly inauspicious. In fact, as Sennett commented later, "No matter what we called it, the film was a flop."

The character burlesqued by Chaplin in the initial handful of releases was that of a traditional British fop. His garb, an oxford gray cutaway, checked waistcoat, batwing collar, polka-dot tie and top hat, was the same he had employed on the stage. Unhappy with his own performances and the fierce competition from the balance of the company, he began experimenting with clothing, on the theory that clothes make the clown. First he borrowed a pair of the out-sized Arbuckle trousers. Then he filched Ford Sterling's old shoes. Wtihin minutes these items, plus derby and cane, were assembled into a ridiculous but magically unified ensemble—and the screen's greatest figure, the Little Tramp, was born.

In a tryout of the new character, conceived to fit the costume, Chaplin jogged over to a hotel lobby set and made like a drunk. Chester Conklin, who aided and abetted the transformation, tells about this sneak preview:

He got his foot caught in the cuspidor. His cane betrayed him and tripped him up. The mustache wiggled like a rabbit's nose. A crowd gathered. Mabel and Hank and Avery and Arbuckle were laughing at Charlie. We didn't notice that the Old Man had come down from his tower and was standing in the rear. All of a sudden we heard him. "Chaplin, you do exactly what you're doing now in your next picture. Remember to do it in that get up. Otherwise, dear old England is beckoning."

The characterization was, of course, an instantaneous success. Chaplin's Charlie the Tramp became the most distinctive comedy figure at the Edendale lot, diminutive alongside such giants as Arbuckle and Swain, yet in a way bigger than any of them.

Relying more on his own instinctive timing and the insertion of bizarre actions than on the established Keystone gags (which he had always found alien to his taste), Chaplin appeared only once in a pie-throwing orgy (*Dough and Dynamite*), never with the Bathing Beauties and seldom in an auto chase. "He was always a fugitive," Sennett remarked, adding: "A *furtive* fugitive." From his tenth picture forward, the ex-music hall pantomimist—about whom everyone had had serious second thoughts—received writing and directing credit, which reveals the personal stamp he set upon even his early efforts.

The first eleven Tramp comedies (also starring Mabel Normand) brought the characterization through its first important phase. Sennett felt that nothing new was added afterwards. "Though in the process of shrinking his tramp to pathetic and lovable proportions, it was a long time before he abandoned cruelty, venality, treachery, larceny and lechery as the main characteristics." In *Her Friend the Bandit* Charlie plays an impostor who visits Mabel's fancy mansion and, out of frustration, tears it apart. In *Mabel's Busy Day* Charlie gets drunk in a saloon and steals hot dogs from a poor girl who operates a small sidewalk stand. He bankrupts her. In *Mabel's Married Life* he staggers home in an alcoholic daze and is defeated in a boxing match with a dummy. *A Gentleman of Nerve* shows him sneaking through a hole in a fence, for the purpose of watching an auto race; after managing to get several innocent people arrested, he winds up as a thief. Preceding W. C. Fields by many years, Charlie got laughs in *His Trysting Place* by threatening to strangle a baby. Nowhere could a cockier, pluckier, more sadistic, violent, criminous and totally uninhibited clown be apprehended in that period.

As the characterization grew, however, many of these traits were smoothed out, eliminated or combined. Taking his cue from the great French comic Max Linder (who graciously denied that he had ever taught "Charlot" anything), Chaplin added the quality of wistfulness. It was the final touch. Sennett offered his star one-half of his own one-third interest in Keystone, but Charlie declined. He moved to Essanay Studios in Chicago, starting at an incredible $1,250 per week. A year later he commanded $10,000 per week and a bonus of $150,000 per year from Mutual, becoming the highest paid theatrical performer in the world.

The Little Fellow's subsequent rise to the highest peaks of artistry is known to all. It should be remembered, though, that his first home, Keystone, his foster father, Mack Sennett, and his fellow orphan inmates were all vital factors in the creation.

Surprisingly, it was a woman who set the wacky tone of the day. Irrepressible madcap Mabel Normand, who looked like the standard innocent-eyed heroine and behaved like a female Keystone Cop, was (in Sennett's words) "our mainstay." She taught Chaplin his first turns. She thought up gags for all the other comics. She threw the first pie, in an ad lib sequence, opening the way for a million sticky laughs. Once she jumped into a lake twenty-two times in order to achieve the right effect. Working hard, playing hard, living for the Edendale fun house and its insane product, she was the very spirit of comedy.

Her chapter in the history of slapstick opens with the blazing succession of Keystone mortgage lifters, with Chaplin, Ben Turpin, Chester Conklin and Fatty Arbuckle, and closes on a tragic note: her involvement in the William Desmond Taylor murder of the twenties.

Molly-O, an ambitious feature concocted by Sennett's gagmen, or scenarists, was on the shelf, ready for release, when Taylor—a motion-picture director known more for his amorous adventures than for his cinematic talents—was shot to death by person or persons unknown. Mabel and Mary Miles Minter were among this gentleman's last visitors. Although no accusations were leveled, the association was sufficient to bring down the wrath of the self-appointed guardians of the nation's morals. Sennett was forced to withdraw *Molly-O,* losing half a million dollars. Mabel, described by all who knew her as the kindest, sweetest, most lovable person in the business—Mabel, the bright, zany incarnation of fun—was drummed out of pictures and propelled toward a hard and early death.

The need for extreme discretion was pointed up by this incident, but the clown mask is not so easy to slip off. Most of the public-relations problems that dogged the stars of the silent comedies stemmed from their wholesale zest for living and the ready acceptance, by their friends, of anything they might care to do. The need to top one's previous performance, whether in public or private, pushes a certain type of actor to the heights. Conversely it drags him to the depths. All the great film clowns, with the exception of Harold Lloyd, suffered from private tragedy and public abuse.

Surely none suffered more than Roscoe "Fatty" Arbuckle. He was a big, jolly, mischievous man who played big, jolly, mischievous men on the screen. The world loved him. His peers bowed to him as one of the greatest comedians of all time. It is not recorded that he had a single enemy. Yet one night's indiscretion destroyed him and his image and his memory. It happened at the St. Francis hotel, in San Francisco. Arbuckle was hosting another of his well-known open-house parties. Girls were present, including a sturdy Hollywood hopeful named Virginia Rappe. The newspapers described her later as a "frail, lovely virgin." Buster Keaton says that she was ". . . a big-boned, husky young woman, five feet, seven inches tall, who weighed 135 pounds . . . about as virtuous as most of the other untalented young women who had been knocking around Hollywood for years, picking up small parts any way they could." In the course of the party the actress suffered a "pelvic disturbance." Within a few hours she was dead.

The courts tried Arbuckle for manslaughter and judged him innocent. The great world public, however, was not so lenient. Roscoe's fans condemned him. No longer was he the funny fat man who filled their hearts with joy. Now he was an obese, gross, lecherous monster whose lustful bulk tore the insides out of an innocent young girl. (Actually, three versions of the incident were in office and alley circulation: Arbuckle had raped the girl, killing her with thrusts of his presumably enormous penis; he had used a Coca-Cola bottle as a dildo; he had impaled her on a broom handle. Most people devoutly believed all three stories.)

It was the blackest, ugliest page in show-business history. Fatty Arbuckle was driven out of motion pictures. After two decades of success and fame, the jolly clown—mentor to Keaton, innovator of a thousand priceless gags, dispenser of delight to millions—was summarily consigned to disgrace, obscurity and neglect. Years later, when the scandal had faded, Roscoe tried a comeback. But the memory of mobs shouting obscenities at him in the name of Reform stifled the big man's urge to play the buffoon; and when we might have been treated once again to his art, the clown was dead.

Buster Keaton's tragedy was almost as great. His fans never deserted him. Now, because of his activities in television, he is probably the most familiar of the silent-screen comics. Yet he had a twenty-year-long bout with obscurity and despair.

The poker-faced, basset-eyed, loose-knit Keaton we know today differs only in age and sagging jowls from the poker-faced, basset-eyed, loose-knit four-year-old who was knocking them dead in 1899. The youngster worked into his parents' act by becoming a heckler. Shortly afterward he joined his father in a rough-and-tumble acrobatic altercation that gave great pain to the Society for the Prevention of Cruelty to Children, if not to Buster. So adept at avoiding fractures did the pair become that the elder Keaton often forgot that his son was not an oddly-shaped missile to be thrown about at will. On one occasion he actually used the child as a weapon, hurling him into the audience at a third-row cutup who had become obnoxious.

This tender training, plus an inborn sense of comic effect, supplied The Human Projectile with all the necessary attributes for slapstick films. When the family act broke up, he went to work at the Colony Studios in Brooklyn, owned and operated by the newly independent Fatty Arbuckle.

Buster's debut was made in an Arbuckle epic called *The Butcher Boy*. His first moment of glory comes as he enters the country store where most of the action takes place. Fatty and Al St. John, the proprietors, are engaged (naturally enough) in throwing bags of flour at each other. Buster walks accidentally into the line of fire. He takes a bag full in the face. His blank expression following the assault is such a contrast to the fevered eyeball-rollings and open mouths of the other comedians that an extra dimension had been brought to insanity. Throughout the film—during which he must remove a quarter from a full pail of molasses and endure the bite of a mangy hound—Keaton maintains his carved-from-granite calm. Once established, this deadpan became his trademark. No one ever managed to copy it successfully.

The late James Agee, also belatedly appreciated, described Keaton's face as "ranking almost with Lincoln's as an early American archetype, haunting, handsome, almost beautiful." Once it was so. Buster's early movies reveal him as a sensitive-featured young man, with many of the same elements of inner pathos and compassion that distinguished Chaplin. Like Chaplin, his characterizations depicted the victim of circumstances rather than the gossoon who violates propriety. Hence there was a certain nobility and grandeur to his clowning.

The Deadpan was frequently as funny and inventive as the Tramp, occasionally more so. Yet even Keaton's staunchest fans will admit that he lacked the greatness of Chaplin, if only because of the necessary limitations of the frozen-face characterization. Still, if there ever was a challenger to Charlie's throne, it was Buster Keaton.

He was a natural jester but he was (and is) a serious student of humor, also. Tension/growth-of-tension/release-of-tension was his formula, and it saw him through some of the funniest movies ever made, notably *The General* (recently revived for television), *Go West* and *The Navigator*. He was called a director, but he didn't direct. He choreographed and danced the leading role in over a hundred screen ballets, any one of which would intimidate the Moiseyev Company.

The ex-acrobat scorned the use of doubles and so suffered more bruises, abrasions, contusions, black eyes and fractures (including a broken neck) than all the other comics put together. Buster's sight-gags almost always relied upon physical contact between man and object. In one two-reeler he dives from a high board into a swimming pool, misses the water and crashes through the tile coping. In *One Week* he puts up a prefabricated house in a completely hopeless fashion, steps outside the misplaced door to admire his work—and falls two stories. Yet Keaton was capable of subtlety, too. His well-paced, well-thought-out pictures were amalgams of the loud and the soft, the wild and the pensive, the obvious and the subtle.

With the advent of sound, Buster came under the aegis of M-G-M and its youthful production supervisor, Irving Thalberg. Unwilling to assign the veteran comic his own unit for fear other stars would demand similar dispensation, Thalberg unwittingly started Keaton on his long downhill slide. "He thought he was doing the right thing," Buster recalls. "And you couldn't say he was stingy. I got as many as twenty-two writers for every script. But that was the trouble. Everything had to be on paper." The Organization Idea, dominant in Hollywood today but only beginning then, stifled Keaton's sense of spontaneity. With "help" from everyone at the studio, he soon retreated into frustration and inactivity. Compounded by a matrimonial disaster, his fortunes declined to a point where he was happy to accept work at $100 per week in the studio where once he had commanded $200,000 per year. Some bits in big films and a willingness to try the fledgling medium, TV, brought the great Deadpan back to his admirers, in small but thoroughly enjoyable doses. He is not the star he used to be—that would be impossible, in any case—but neither is he a pathetic relic. As one of Hollywood's senior citizens, who made the most difficult transition imaginable without losing either his hope or his sense of values, Buster Keaton treasures the plaudits of his fans and their affectionate memory of the "little man with the frozen face who made them laugh a bit long years ago when they and I were both young."

For others there was no transition at all. "Talkies" spelled the end of many great careers and the beginning of the end of an entire age.

Suddenly there was no more call for Larry Semon, a direct descendant of Dan Leno and all the great flour-faced European clowns; for Harry Langdon, the bewildered babe-in-the-woods with the survival instincts of an Apache; for cross-eyed Ben Turpin; bumbling Andy Clyde; indestructible Chester Conklin; no call at all for the prancing, dancing mimes whose silent frenzies convulsed the world. The expression of Everyman's distrust of his environment and his defiance of Fate through the lifted eyebrows and waggling backsides of shadow-figures ceased to be. The new talking toy called for, not a new expression necessarily, but a new method.

Semon, who died the year sound was fully adapted for the screen, had actually been in retirement for a number of years. But if he had tried to find employment in the profession at which he was an acknowledged master, it is certain that he would have failed. The barrier was understandably oak-strong at the time. In the embryonic development of sound film, dubbing had not been perfected. Therefore all scenes were required to be shot complete with whatever sound effects were desired in the finished print. The sound camera, noisy in itself, was necessarily shrouded and limited in movement. The sets, accordingly, were small and totally sealed against random decibels. So action—the heart of comedy—was circumscribed. And this alone, without the other limitations brought by sound, killed the knockabout, Keystone type of movie.

Classic motion-picture slapstick struggled to stay alive. Harold Lloyd fought the coming revolution with a series of silent masterpieces, any one of which should have been adequate to stem the flood of words. Chaplin delivered his finest gifts. Keaton, at the peak of his powers, tossed off one brilliant comedy after another. Indeed, it may be said that the threat of extinction spurred those early practitioners of the art of silent mirth to their greatest accomplishments. The year it died, slapstick comedy was at last truly an art.

Of course, film comedy, in the broad and unspecialized sense, did not die. While most of the great mimes vanished, a new breed of comic sprang up. They were not clowns in the classic sense, nor purely cinematic creations, but a number of them were highly talented and a few—only a few—managed to be so funny that it appeared, for a little while, that a new art was in the making.

The two real giants of this transitional period came very close to merging silent and sound techniques, an impossible blend. Sound creates the illusion of reality; slapstick requires the reality of illusion. Nonetheless Stan Laurel and Oliver Hardy made the attempt, and in so doing contributed a special, peculiar and altogether wonderful form of humor.

The comics were first brought together by a leg of lamb. Laurel, once Chaplin's understudy, was directing silent comedies for Hal Roach when it happened that Hardy, who pursued a gastronomical hobby, suffered third-degree burns in the process of cooking lamb and was forced to miss a scheduled film appearance. Laurel substituted. Roach liked the bit and suggested that the two team up in forthcoming productions. The magic of the combination was at once apparent.

After establishing themselves in the soundless flickers, the delicate hippo Hardy and childlike Laurel moved smoothly into the new medium. Accounting for the transition, Laurel says:

We had decided we weren't talking comedians and of course preferred to do pantomime like in our silents. So, we said as little as possible—only what was necessary to motivate the things we were doing. If there was any plot to be told we generally would have somebody else tell it. We used sound chiefly for the effects and after a while, we really liked sound because it emphasized the gags and eventually we did more talking than we had intended.

Even in their final efforts Laurel and Hardy depended upon the "kaleidoscope of visual images" rather than spoken humor, which ought to have made them misfits, but didn't. Whoever saw the two of them struggling with a grand piano on a swaying rope bridge, with a gorilla coming from the opposite direction; or devouring an invisible dinner in the mansion of a madwoman; or strutting along a forty-story-high scaffolding, both, plus a large live crab, in the same pair of trousers—whoever watched Laurel react to perplexity with his hair-mussing scratch of the head and baby-wrinkled, verge-of-weeping-hysteria face, or Hardy in his ponderous yet graceful attempts to salvage human dignity from the most absurd situations—whoever laid eyes on the colorful, lovable pair at work, brushed with comedy at its finest.

Hardy, known to his friends always as Babe, is gone. Laurel, in poor physical health but mentally sound, lives in a small apartment in Santa Monica, California. It is pleasant to report that, although he remembers the past fondly and vividly, he is primarily interested in the future.

A man who claimed to have been born without a future was W. C. Fields, one of the funniest and most enigmatic figures in motion-picture history. He made his debut as the Ringmaster in the second version of *Tillie's Punctured Romance* but, paradoxically—for he was at heart a mime—he did not achieve renown until after the advent of sound. Although people remember him best for his sly, insouciant, minor-key carny barker's drawl, his finest moments relied not upon sound but sight. He lacked Sennett's innocence—in fact, frequently he appeared to be parodying the style of his mentor—still, he put the Keystone touch in most of his wild extravaganzas. And they were wild. The bulb-nosed misanthrope simply progressed by a nebulous story line from one improbable situation to the next, disregarding with Olympian contempt the careful plotting and attempted logic of competitive products. His people and their activities: the inventor of a puncture-proof tire who flattens all the casings on a police car by gunfire, under the impression it is his test vehicle; the intrepid game hunter who is terrified by any four-legged creature and runs from a pair of tame lions; the pool shark who is forced to play with a corkscrewlike cue—these and other grotesque characterizations, presumably disparate, all blended into one dumpy, suspicious, ill-tempered, dishonest, cowardly, and somehow magnificent fool. No one ever claimed that Fields was lovable. But no one who saw the incredibly nihilistic car chase in *The Bank Dick,* or the scene in *Never Give a Sucker an Even Break* where Fields accidentally drops a bottle of whiskey from an airplane and dives unhesitatingly after it, sans parachute, no witness of his almost nightmarish humor could deny that he was a great comic.

Equally great, and very definitely outgrowths of the sound period, were three brothers who were born with the gift of madness and a sense that the world was a laugh: the brothers Marx. More than merely a team of comics, Groucho, with his suggestive, *reductio ad absurdum* eyebrows, his idiot slump-shouldered walk and his habit of saying whatever happened to be on his mind; Harpo, the Panlike angel-devil; and their foil, Chico, combined three separate schools of comedy into a spicy, meaty, sometimes unidentifiable porridge remembered well by all who loved film humor. There was almost no sweetness to the brothers. They were not quaint nor charming nor appealing. Often they were obnoxious. But always they were funny; and if there was a certain desperation to their lunatic activities, it was only because they were destined to be the last of the Great Destroyers, the last recognizable link to old-time slapstick.

After the Marx Brothers, American comedy suffered a swift and inexorable decline. There were comics and funny pictures, to be sure, but they were a break from tradition, following no pattern and achieving little art. The Ritz Brothers, Joe Penner, Hugh Herbert, Leon Erroll, Joe E. Brown, Eddie Cantor, Olsen and Johnson, and others frequently hit high standards; but somehow they all seemed out of context. Their humor gradually grew tame, controlled, almost polite. And in time they, too, disappeared.

The "American renascence" with Abbott and Costello, Martin and Lewis, Bob Hope, et al., was, of course, no such thing. It was the feeble twitch of a dying giant.

Now we have exactly two clowns, and they are lost, out of time, out of step, and aging. Danny Kaye, an artful exhibitionist, began well but, like Keaton, was soon crushed by the Hollywood machinery. The gigantic, Technicolor, wide-screen bushel baskets under which he is obliged to hide the light of his talent are uniformly spiritless and unrewarding. Red Skelton is with us, but only in spirit, which is just as well. The inestimable Red never was meant to work in films or TV. Stepping back centuries to Grimaldi and the white-faced jesters, he exists as an anachronism and a reminder, in semihuman form, of a past art.

There are no others. Slapstick is gone from the American screen, brutally murdered by sound, growing sophistication and a wonderful, but undistinguished, toy called the animated cartoon. Of this sub-art Gene Fowler commented: "It preserved and accentuated a thousand-fold all the illusions of slapstick. The pen was mightier than the bed slat. By the exercise of a few thousand strokes of the cartoonist's quill, a whole animal kingdom of stars came into being and had immortal existence. . . ."

Mickey Mouse, Donald Duck, Bugs Bunny, and the other inkwell stars drew no salaries, never became temperamental, suffered no stains of public misdemeanor, and were wholly unlikely to succumb to ulcers and coronaries. Combined with the assault of the talking double feature, they delivered the *coup de grâce* to slapstick as it was practiced by the masters. Yet they did not replace or take over slapstick, even though they borrowed its methods. One is not surprised to see a five-foot-high mouse do anything, and surprise was an essential ingredient in the art.

Ironically, the nations who never had a look-in when America was King are now the arbiters of film comedy. Alec Guinness, Terry-Thomas and Peter Sellers in Britain; Fernandel and Jacques Tati in France; Cantinflas in Mexico—all are nibbling on the fringes of great comedic style, and it is to them that we must look for a return of laughter.

Perhaps it would be well for us to think about that.

Perhaps, as the young man scratches our consciousness from the grooves of a vinyl disc, it would be well for us to rediscover the slap shoes and funny hat we were born with, and the admirable and defiant mirth which was our legacy. It is not too late. In fact, the fearful absurdity is only beginning, waiting to be laughed into its proper place.

The undead

IT WAS an unusually gusty day for California in that Spring of 1952, but I didn't question the wind. Nor would I have questioned a sky gone suddenly black with the flight of bats, in thousands, quarking dire alarms; or a stillness upon the streets, broken only by an occasional far-off scream; or even angry mobs of villagers bearing heavy knobkerries sharpened to points. These things would have frightened me, but I would not have questioned them. For I was on my way to see Count Dracula.

My agent of that period had telephoned me at 3:00 A.M. with the news that one of my stories had been read with enthusiasm by Bela Lugosi. The actor had begun the yarn in the midnight hours (as when else?) and had shortly afterward contacted the agent. Would it be possible, he wondered, for the author to pay him a personal call, to discuss terms? And . . . would Mr. Beaumont please come alone?—he disliked crowds; they made him jumpy.

Not wishing to make Mr. Lugosi jumpy, I agreed on both counts, and soon found myself trudging through odd hillside streets toward an unfamiliar address. With each step, the years seemed to peel away. I began to resurrect long-buried memories. Lugosi as the paranoiac commander of a school of blind men; Lugosi as Baron von Frankenstein's hunchbacked assistant, Ygor, torturing the helpless Monster; then, later, becoming this Monster and being tortured by others; a hundred flash recollections of Lugosi stabbing and throttling and smothering, and biting, walking the screens as the personification of all the goblin evils that ever were; and, finally, in his royal cloak and deathly pallor, Lugosi as the greatest fiend of them all.

As I checked the numbers off the apartment houses and knew I was coming close, it occurred to me that here was the Compleat Bogeyman. Karloff was a better actor, and so were Rathbone and Lorre, but we had seen them all with their horror-masks off. We knew they were human beings. Karloff had edited fine anthologies of supernatural stories (*And the Darkness Falls, Tales of Terror*), so brilliantly done that one could no longer think of him as a *bona fide* monster, and Lorre and Rathbone, tiring of grue, had returned to straight roles—to the vast disappointment of such addicts of vintage horror as myself.

Lugosi, however, remained true to the cause. His roles were invariably grotesque, and even (as in *The Body Snatchers*) when he might have played it "straight," he chose otherwise.

He was a bat, a corpse, a cripple, a creature, a cheat, a thief, a murderer, an animal, a mad professor; but he was never, never a normal human being.

Musing thus and expecting a Transylvanian castle or, at the

very least, a shabby, time-gnarled house, I was somewhat surprised to discover a California-style apartment unit, all chrome
and pink plaster and dichondra. There was, I'm afraid, a swimming pool, but it had no water in it, and that was encouraging.

I stood for a delicious moment, feeling a bit like Dwight
Fry and a bit like the boy who saw *Island of Lost Souls* and
went home and could not sleep for two nights; then I knocked.

Count Dracula opened the door. He was very old and weak,
his flesh was parchmented, and he held a cigar in his left hand;
but it was *he,* unmistakably.

"You are Mister Beaumont?" he asked; and his voice was
as rich and alien as ever, his smile as darkly inviting.

I shook his hand and went inside. The apartment was in
chaos. It was full of trunks and mismatched furniture and rugs
and curios.

"I have read your story, Mister Beaumont. I want to come
back to the screen, in the role of your devil."

I'd forgotten that Mr. Lugosi had not appeared in a film
for many years. I told him I would be very proud of the distinction.

He leaned forward. "You have seen my movies?"

"All of them," I said. "Some of them three and four times."

"Indeed?"

He put the cigar in his mouth and grinned happily. Then
he gestured toward the wall. It was covered by a gigantic painting. "That is myself," he said, "as Count Dracula."

It was a surprisingly good painting, unsigned, beginning to
crack. It portrayed Lugosi as a young man, clad in the familiar
evening suit and cloak. He was handsome and lithe and every
inch a vampire.

He laughed. "Myself." He shook his head and began to reminisce, speaking only of his tours with Dracula, what the role meant to him, how he had come to associate himself with the character.

"I made a great deal of money in those days," he said. "But now I do not have any money. In fact, I am looking for someone to share this apartment with me. Not because of the money. Because I am lonely."

I thought of sleeping in the same apartment with Bela Lugosi, particularly with the moon full, and the night windy. . . .

"About your story," he said, and we began to talk business. It evolved that he could not pay me but that if we went to a certain studio, now, we could undoubtedly raise the cash. "The producer there," he said, "worked on many pictures with me. He is a friend. He will give us the cash."

We got into my car—an ancient Lincoln—and started toward the studio. Lugosi dreamed aloud. "With this part, I will be number one again," he said. "I know it." He fell silent and remained so until a small dog strolled into the street a full block ahead. Lugosi sat forward. "Don't hit the dog!" he shrieked. "You fool!"

I slowed to twenty miles per hour. The animal crossed safely. Lugosi patted his forehead with a handkerchief.

"Listen," he said, snorting. "Listen: right after *Dracula,* they called me and asked, did I wish to play in a picture called *Frankenstein.* When they told me about the part, I said: 'I am a star. I will not take a role without dialogue!' So I called a friend of mine in New York. He was starving. I told him the part was nothing, but perhaps he would make a little money. He came to Hollywood. He made the picture. Now Boris

Karloff is on top and I am on the bottom. It is very funny."

I learned many years later from Karloff that he met Lugosi for the first time when they appeared together in the second *Frankenstein* picture, and that he got the role of the Monster as the result of a producer's happening to notice him in the studio commissary. But even if I'd realized my companion was lying, I'd have felt sad. Because he shouldn't have been on the bottom.

We stopped at the studio and Lugosi got out of the car.

I waited for an hour; then he came back, looking tired.

"He will not give us any money," he said. "Please take me home."

I took him home. He thanked me for my trouble, apologized for the inconvenience, and pressed my hand. I went away.

I knew nothing of his addiction to narcotics at that time, nor did I have any hint of his marital difficulties. I only knew that, for me, Dracula was finally dead, and in his place was a sick, friendless, lonely old man. . . .

The old man made one final appearance in the film *The Black Sleep;* then, on the seventeenth of August, 1956, he, too, died.

His last wish was that his famous black cloak be draped across his body and buried with him. This was done.

Lament for
the high iron

THERE WERE giants upon the earth when the earth was young. Enormous fire-breathing giants they were, with voices of thunder and a tireless stride that carried them across continents. And people feared them, because they were the most powerful creatures that ever existed; but people loved them, too, for they served man.

The creatures were called trains. They are not gone from the earth yet, but they are going. Inexorably, they are passing into extinction, like the giants of another time, the dinosaurs. Yet they will never be forgotten. Like the dinosaurs, they also will pass into legend. And, one day, a hundred thousand years from now, a schoolboy will be asked to describe this time of ours and he will begin an essay titled *The Railroad Age*.

If the essay is thorough, it will open with a study of America, for this country owes its existence to railroads. Over a period of almost a century and a half, our land was a veritable webwork of railroads, of main lines and short lines, of standard- and narrow-gauge lines: a reticulum of steel ribbons along which rushed the mighty iron monsters—and they were the corpuscles in the lifeblood of our continent. If they had stopped, the arteries would have collapsed and America would have withered and died. That is how important they were.

The past tense is shocking, but only slightly premature. While our eyes are on the jets, the missiles and the space capsules, the glory and the grandeur that was railroading is quietly fading from the contemporary scene. Unimaginable but true that all the lore, the romance and vivid lexicon of an era will utterly vanish, and all in our lifetime; that for a while, before it is elevated by heraldry, the train will be consigned to the Quaint Artifact section of the museum, somewhere between the Conestoga wagon and the oxcart.

So let us sing the giants to their rest now, while yet they can hear us; and let us sing loudly, without tears, if we can. We are not, after all, mourning a sickly friend whose face we have forgotten, nor sighing for a bit of childhood lost: the song is for giants.

Think of them. Think of how it was when you went down to the depot to see the One-O-Four, not because It Was There but because it would be, soon. Remember how you walked the track, pretending it was a hundred feet up, and tried not to fall, and did. How you knelt and put your ear to the steel and waited. For miles ahead nothing could be seen but the diminishing tracks, but you knew it was coming, and you went on waiting. Any moment. Now! The steel began to vibrate. You looked up; still nothing in sight; then back down, quick, bare ear pressed against bare steel, and the vibration turning into a hum. You could hear it truly. Another couple of moments ("Get the hell away from there, boy! You wanta get yourself killed?") and up, scrambling over the cindery gravel. Still nothing ahead. Then a far-off scream and a black dot, and your heart beginning to jump. The One-O-Four! Another shrill scream, the dot becoming larger, taking on shape, the rails shaking, the ground trembling, and you, edging just as close to the track as your courage allowed. Watching the great iron beast approaching, you felt again the crazy urge to throw yourself in front of it, but you only felt this for a split second, just long enough to be thrilled. No time for anything else, anyway, because here it was, thundering past you, great wheels turning, pistons pumping, brakes screeching, and you were lost in a pure white cloud of joy and warm steam.

The province into which the One-O-Four moved was yours, but you were humbled. You'd stand there in the middle of the open, staring at the strange people—strange because you had never seen them before and you would never see them again—and they would stare back, as aristocrats in a peasant land: patronizingly, pityingly, scornfully; or so you fancied. Those in the dining car gazed out with a particularly jaundiced eye, seeing you not at all but, instead, the distance, beyond this unimportant town, beyond you and all that made up the world you lived in. You often wondered if they even knew the name of the town. And you hated them a little for their obvious superiority, and this made you want to throw a stone lightly at the window to attract their attention, to let them know that you, too, somehow counted in the scheme of things. But you never did this. They were the gods, the lucky ones, these diners, sitting before tables covered with whitest linen and sparkling silver, with the shapes of waiters hovering at their sides. They were a people apart moving from one Olympus to another, people from a world apart, people from a world you'd never know, from another time and another place, people who started their soup fifty miles up the line and would finish their last cup of coffee fifty miles down the line. Where were they going, and where did they come from? And by what right did they move into town, bisecting it with a railroad car, stopping traffic and commerce? Of course, you knew. They did it by the Divine Right of Railroads, for they were, in this brief passage, part of the railroad, and as such they were immune from the ordinary rules of life.

You thought these things if you lived in a town where the trains stopped. And you thought more: When the mighty high-wheeler at the head end gave two long blasts of its whistle and the heavy steel wheels began to turn, the immense train moved, proud and defiant; to the accompaniment of angry clouds of smoke and steam, it moved, down the track, and dwindled into the mysterious distances; and your heart moved with it, for you'd made the promise again. Some day you would be an aristocrat. Some day you would sit at that table and stare out at the poor kids. But you'd remember to smile and, maybe, if you felt expansive, step outside and shake their hands.

How different this was from those occasions when you would hike over to the airport! From a world of regularity and *establishment* to one of near madness. No schedules here, no certainty. You might see something and you might not; it depended, for the most part, on the whims and caprices of a few daredevil fliers; if the weather wasn't right, your long walk was for nothing. There was always the hope, though, that you might see a stunting airplane or two. You might even go up, at two dollars per fifteen minutes, for a view of the town at a thousand feet. That was fun, the first time. The second time, you began to wonder what would happen if that single engine conked out. There was seldom a third time. It took too much nerve, and nerve was the prerequisite for all aerial sorties. No one dreamed of taking such things for granted; it would be like dozing in the front seat of a roller coaster. For there were no guarantees whatever in what was then the risky aeronautical world, the world where there were no planes or airplanes, just aeroplanes, where the stunters were aerialists undifferentiated from trapeze performers who specialized in the flying return, and the pilots were only beginning to be called aviators.

Flying was for the wildly adventurous—or for the very rich, who bought great clumsy-looking crafts and kept them in the hangar. And as you watched, the best time being sunshiny Saturdays and Sundays, you saw the ugly engined crates jounce lumberingly by, their wings shuddering and bending, eventually wavering between earth and sky, belonging to neither, and then, amazingly, move upward in a great noisy spasm. You weren't envious of the pilot or passenger, despite your ambitions to become another Baron von Richthofen. There were many thoughts, many feelings, but one thing you surely did not consider: that one day somewhat modified versions of the bloodless birds you were watching would, in partnership with trucks, buses, passenger cars and improved hard roads, all but destroy the venerable institution of train travel.

In fact, if you had *any* thoughts about the future of train travel, they were to the effect that it was here to stay. The sight of giant locomotives roaring across the countryside, trailing their pearled plumes, with a cut of fifty cars in tow, or more—

this was so commonplace, their thunderous snorts in heavy labor so ordinary, their polyglot whistles so much a part of the American scene, that you did not bother to appreciate them consciously. It was only the children who stood and wondered. They were always let out of school once a year and escorted down to the station for a close look at the leviathans, and invariably they stood in awe of what they saw: a black looming mass of high iron capable of achieving whatever it chose to, a taller-than-the-tallest-house colossus, with its human masters, or servants, in attendance. There was the striped uniform of the engineer, the bandana neckerchief, the bright copper oil-can; and the man himself, looking every wrinkle and seam the King. There were the brakemen with their flashlights, examining the wheels and boxes, as though anything could ever go wrong. And there, the shiny dark-blue-suited conductors with their omnipresent railroad watches, to which they continually referred, and by which the world kept time; and the red lanterns they always carried, if they were at the rear of the train, signaling mysteriously to the engineer. These were not sights for you; you were older than the children, very blasé, for you had seen it all many times before. Still, did you ever become too old, too blasé? No, indeed; it was merely that your pleasure had been deepened, moving from brain to blood.

Certainly you would never be so old that you would not thrill to the moment when, in response to the chuffing of the engine, the coach you were in started to move, almost imperceptibly, gaining speed, the train snaking its channeled way precisely out of the yards and into the wide, bright world.

Didn't you always press your forehead against the already smudged glass the better to see the old buildings go by, the ones with the car wheels and the lanterns, the signal lights and the switches, to watch the towers and poles glide by until you were truly out in the country, rolling along, lulled by the satisfying clickety-clack of the rails and the Doppler effect of the clanging railroad-crossing signals? On warm days, when the windows were open, you might even get a cinder in your eye, or draw into your nostrils a whiff of the sulphurated smoke direct from the monster's throat.

You didn't care: the dream had come true: you were an aristocrat now.

The railroads were at their zenith then, and time was standing still. Their proud engines and cars displayed heralds that were bywords of the day: Santa Fe, Rock Island, Great Northern, Union Pacific, Southern Pacific, Great Western, the Chicago, Burlington & Quincy, Baltimore & Ohio, Missouri-Kansas-Texas, Denver & Rio Grande, the Atchison, Topeka & Santa Fe —the list is endless, each name distinct and more stately than the last. Even the trains themselves were adding color to the literature: Twentieth Century Limited, Hiawatha, City of San Francisco, Broadway Limited, Panama Limited, Super Chief, Sunshine Special, Capitol Limited, Sunset. And the cars that made up the trains: *Pocahontas, Blue Feather, Helena Modjeska, Prince Rupert, Rose Creek.*

Poets were inspired to sonnets by these names, and novelists put them into their books, just for the music of them. But it took a giant to write properly of the giants, and he did. Over and over again Tom Wolfe plunged his great hands into the lore and brought out gold, as though he knew that this was the crest of the wave, this time, a culmination of all that had been high adventure, the beginning of the end of the color and romance that had seen through the years a flowering of wheel and track, a century of ever-reaching fingers of steel across the country, over the fields of her, into the valleys, through the very mountains. Now there were steam engines capable of running at speeds in excess of a hundred miles an hour with complete safety, trains that could take curves at seventy without spilling more than a few drops of your coffee, trains that passed each other as a matter of routine at speeds over ninety, the point of passing brief and savage, an instant's blurred lightning bolt that for this moment obscured the onrushing scenery and set your heart rapping.

The beginning of the end? Ridiculous thought. Why, the trains were modernizing all the time, streamlining, and there was the Diesel-electric on the horizon. The golden age of railroading had only just begun, we told ourselves. And it seemed so.

The country could point with pride to the New York Central's Twentieth Century Limited, probably the most famous train in all the world, powered by a locomotive described as a Hudson-type Class J-3A, which developed a cylinder horsepower of 4,700 at seventy-five miles per hour, a completely air-conditioned beauty, all rooms de luxe, with a bar lounge, two diners, and an observation-lounge car. This was the train for which the long red carpet was laid at Grand Central Station and at LaSalle Street in Chicago. This was the train that represented an investment of $1,384,000 and made its run of 960 miles from New York to Chicago at an average of a mile a minute including stops. That was luxury *and* speed, and there was an army to see to it that both were maintained—eight enginemen, eight firemen, three conductors, six brakemen, three baggagemen, a train secretary, barber, tailor and maid, one Pullman conductor and as many porters as sleeping cars. The two dining cars had a crew of twenty-four. This was a train that, in the forty years of its running, brought in more than $142,000,000. Where else could it go, with its constant improvements, but on to bigger and better things?

There were other great lines, some fit to challenge the Twentieth Century, or, for that matter, Europe's fabulous *Train Bleu* and Orient Express. The Broadway Limited, for example, was the favorite child of the Pennsylvania System, a speed train, all rooms, offering complete privacy over the shortest east-west route between New York and Chicago with a running time of sixteen hours. The Pennsy had ten great trains between these two cities, six to St. Louis, three to Detroit, seven to Cleveland, twenty-four to Pittsburgh and fifty to Philadelphia every twenty-four hours. The road would offer the Trail Blazer, a low-cost, high-speed train between New York and Chicago with reclining seat coaches, all seats reserved, including observation buffet-lounge cars, club-lounge cars and twin-unit diners with popular-priced meals and refreshments.

The Southern Pacific Company had the Daylight streamliner between San Francisco and Los Angeles, a Saxony red-and-orange train with aluminum striping extending over its entire length, including locomotive and tender. The interiors were of varying color schemes, shades of apricot, jade and Nantes blue, with ceilings of warm ivory. The reclining chairs were upholstered with curly mohair and cushioned with soft sponge-rubber; they could be swiveled to face windows of exceptional width, from which position one could view the Camino Real, which linked the chain of early California missions, the rich Santa Clara valley, the Salinas valley, the Santa Lucía Mountains, and the sheer cliffs and blue waters of the Pacific Ocean for more than a hundred miles.

Wherever you went there were fine trains to take you. The Louisville & Nashville offered the Pan-American and the Azalean between Cincinnati and New Orleans, the Southland and Flamingo (Cincinnati to Atlanta), the Dixie Flyer, the Dixie Limited and the Dixiana (Evansville to Nashville), the Jacksonian and the Florida Arrow (Louisville to Montgomery). There were others: the Crescent, the Piedmont Limited, the Dixie Flagler, the South Wind, and many, many more, all great.

Even freight trains were not excluded from the romance that pervaded all phases of railroading, as a partial sampling of names will show. An all-freight from Columbus to Chicago was called the Big Smoke. Another that moved between Buffalo and Harsimus Cove was known, simply, as Guts. Others bore such euphonious designations as the Speed Witch, the Blue Goose, Cock of the Walk and the Cornucopia.

For every big line, there were hundreds of smaller ones, entirely independent railroads offering passenger service. The Doniphan, Kensett & Searcy in Arkansas ran twice daily between Kensett and Searcy, a distance of six miles. The McCloud River transported people from McCloud to Hambone, a distance of thirty-two California miles. They ran on schedule, these tiny lines, and they made money.

There was all of this, and Diesel-electric around the corner. You thought, Sure, maybe the roads will lose some of their charm with the new engines, and you knew you'd miss the delightful cindery smell of the steamers; but a train was a train, and nothing would ever change that.

With only slight apprehension, you watched the march of progress. Railroads which had kept the status quo for more than twenty years began to modernize. Passenger trains became air-conditioned, lines adopted tight-lock couplings, rubber draft gears, interlocker signal systems and centralized traffic control. They did go to Diesels, most of them, and to streamlining. They grew quieter and smoother. At first the face was unfamiliar, along with the build, but you got used to it. Of course you mourned for the smokestack and that old black magic of the big iron, but you knew that all things must bow before progress. You were happy when, little by little, the roads began to recapture some of their glory and lustre, inching back to the splendor of other years, with super-luxury cars complete with barber shops, motion-picture theatres, doctors, radios, showers, wall-to-wall carpeting, maids and manicurists. There were new cars called "slumber coaches," strata domes and vista domes, passenger cars with names like Silver Lake and Silver Arrow to suggest, if not to match, the Silver Palace Cars of another generation. Progress had not licked trains; it had joined them. Now, available for everyone, were drawing rooms, compartments, double bedrooms, duplex single rooms, roomettes and parlor cars, the last at one time the pinnacle of solid, stately elegance for the daytime rail traveler. For the dreamers, there were, still, the observation platforms, where a man could stand with his head in the wind and his hands about the brass rail and watch the miles clicking away.

Then something happened.

Out of the scrub pine and conifers, the railroads came to the bare top of the long, lovely haul; and the road ahead was not level. It sloped downward in a gently lowering curve, so gentle, so smooth that the passengers did not even know they were descending. Revenues, however, knew very well.

Railroads had always been taxed high; that started when they were young, powerful and wealthy. But when business slackened, restrictive legislation, which had been imposed upon them when they were indeed a monopoly, plus the high taxes, remained; and they were soon losing as much as a million dollars a quarter. Naturally the railroads became frantic. They cut service, after all appeals had been denied. They cut lines. They cut what personnel they could. And they developed an inordinate passion for mergers, dropping branch lines, cars, offices, stations, sidings, yards and whole sections of track. In 1926 the railroads logged 40 billion passenger miles; in 1960, with the population doubled, they toted up only 20 billion, and recorded a deficit in passenger traffic that totaled nearly three-quarters of a billion dollars. The Transportation Act of 1958, which allowed them to abandon service where losses each year could be proved, was too little and too late.

Why did it happen? What caused it?

For the movement of goods, the semi and the truck-trailer were responsible; for passengers, the automobile and the airplane.

That a superior means of transport should develop and, because of its benefits, displace the old, is logical. One cannot argue that trains are still ideal for shipping freight. The facts prove otherwise. But what of the matter of human beings?

That matter, I think, *is* open to argument.

Assuming the destination to be a continent's length away, how does this generation's traveler choose to go? By car, most often. Unless he is in a hurry, he will gas up the family sedan and embark upon what he fancies will be a leisurely, inexpensive, relaxing journey. Of course, he fancies wrong. He will embark upon a journey fraught with danger, taking his chances on clogged highways and city streets, blinding himself to the extravagant price he pays for propelling his vehicle, for fuel and oil, for repairs, for depreciation, for the inevitably frazzled state of his nerves. He thinks nothing of hidden taxes; in fact, he ignores them. He has a compulsion to be self-steered; after all, it's an *auto*mobile he's driving, isn't it? Now he's free, with freedom to go where he will, down that side road, up that hill, into that town with the funny name, and freedom to stop whenever he wishes and wherever and for however long.

Ideally, he's right; practically, it is nonsense.

Today's highway traveler suffers from a complex which reveals itself in his comments at the end of each traveling day: "Covered eight hundred and fifty-two miles today!" (with pride) or "I don't understand it; we've only gone four hundred and twenty miles" (with shame). This complex, even more than the increased traffic congestion, robs him of his touted freedom. He doesn't take that side road, he doesn't go up that hill, and he never finds out about that town with the funny name. Instead, he sits at the wheel of a deadly projectile, his muscles tense and his eyes focused on the concrete road ahead. And even if he could relax and look off for a minute, what would he see before the crash? Advertisements, exhortations to drive carefully, billboards appealing to his

heart, his stomach, his head, his liver, his pride, his faith and
his digestion.

The plane traveler is hardly better off. Whereas the price
in dollars is low, the price in peace of mind is astronomical.
He pretends, this traveler, to take comfort in the statistics, and
will be happy, after claiming that planes are the safest means
of transportation ever invented, to quote them. "You're a lot
better off in the sky than you are on the highway," he will say,
and he will be correct. Statistically. But there will be an edge
to his voice as he tells you of the x-million passenger miles
flown and the mere x-hundreds of fatalities. Perhaps he is
thinking of last week's headline (AIRLINER CRASHES!
ALL PASSENGERS PERISH!), or of the sweat on his palms
when the big jet took off with him aboard; or perhaps he isn't
thinking anything at all. But the edge is there.

Tell these people about trains and they will chuckle and
ask if you are serious. Point out to the driver that he would
save money in the long run, and have far more actual freedom; tell the air traveler that if he is so fond of statistics he
should investigate those regarding train travel—or, better still,
quote them; they're easy to remember: NOT ONE PAS-
SENGER FATALITY IN PULLMAN CAR TRAINS IN
TEN YEARS.

Advise them that on trains they can have utter privacy, if
they wish it, or social intercourse; that they will be living in a
sort of castle away from home, a room on wheels where they
can relax, read, sleep, do anything they want. Shout to them
that a train, unlike an automobile or an airplane, moves in bad
weather and good, it doesn't matter; that ice on the tracks is

no hazard at all. Tell them that they can now look at the face of America, view mountains without the intervening clutter of billboards, look into back alleys and back yards, across fields and valleys. Try to show them that for the first time they can reach their destination truly and completely relaxed, if only they will make a slight adjustment in their thinking; relaxed, refreshed and ready to enjoy themselves.

But don't try with any hope of success. The complexes are too deep, the thinking too rigidly formed. A train trip for the modern man would, after the first hour or so, evoke nothing. He would probably tap his feet with impatience, crack his knuckles, read all the magazines, look at his watch, ruminate that if he'd only used his head and gone by plane he'd be there by now, and hate the idiot who suggested this outmoded rattle-trap. He wouldn't enjoy it.

The principal reason is that modern man has never culti-vated the art of leisure, which used to be acquired on trains and nurtured ever afterward. He almost never finds himself alone with himself for two or three days; certainly never by choice. There is, he thinks, nothing profitable in it. That it could be the most profitable two or three days in his life is unimaginable.

That is why there is rust instead of silver frost on the steel rails. That is why the old depots and stations are boarded up and over-run with weeds. That is why ties are disintegrating, why there are deserted spurs and decaying rolling stock, cor-roded wheels, boilers, tracks, signals, engines, towers and switches. And that is why ghosts walk the right-of-ways, the long, high trestles, the dark, curving tunnels, the empty, for-saken platform out to the semaphore that isn't there any more, waiting, hoping, listening for the melancholy wail of old One-O-Four as she rounds the bend and puts on steam for the grade.

Trains that once were living things, pulsating and vibrant with life, exist now in the minds and hearts of those who knew them. We were profoundly moved by what we saw and heard and experienced, and so were whole communities whose characters were changed by the trains that stopped there, all the financial and personal roots of them going deep into local history and pride.

For that future schoolboy, and his question: What was a railroad, anyway, that it could mean so much?

The Pennsylvania consists of six hundred former short lines, but railroads *in toto* are more than short lines, more than sections of track and engines and equipment. Railroads are songs the ballad-makers sing: *The Wreck of the Old 97, The Wabash Cannonball, In the Baggage Coach Ahead;* songs we used to sing: *The Atchison, Topeka and the Santa Fe* and *The Chattanooga Choo-Choo* and *Alabamy Bound.* A railroad was the smoker up front with its leather seats and strong smell, its floor etched with spittle and its air blue with smoke, where beard-stubbled men in overalls rubbed shoulders with sports and dandies in loud striped suits with gigantic stickpins in their ties, where drummers and brakemen played a few hands of *seven-up* as they dead-headed back home. A railroad was an influence, a maker of public opinion; and it was drama, high and low: *Under the Gaslight, The Ninety and Nine, A Mile a Minute, The Midnight Special, Forty-Five Minutes from Broadway, Twentieth Century* and *The Honeymoon Express.* It was *The Great Train Robbery,* also, and *Night Train* and

Union Pacific. These were dramatic events that nourished the consciousness of trains and travel and are not likely to be forgotten, even if every foot of track is torn up and overgrown with weeds.

But trains *per se* we forget. Today, stress is placed on getting there, on being right, on the profit of a given action, on the IBM, the computer digital, the laser, construction, workmanship, strategy, precision. It is an age of weighing and measuring and proving.

But a train cannot be weighed or measured, nor can anything about it, in terms of the human equation, be proved. How do you reduce an *experience* to black and white and make it something that can be totaled? How do you weigh or measure the human, pleading wail of a train whistle heard on a rainy night, or convey to someone else what it means, or explain why it lured so many out into the world, into trails west, into the big city? How equate the elegance of a brightly lighted diner and the delicious aroma of the coffee being poured there by an immaculately attired waiter, or the way he sure-footedly rocks with the train, like an old sea captain, as he maneuvers down the aisle with a full tray of soup bowls? And how, in the name of Progress, do you analyze the slumbering quiet of a Pullman sleeper at three in the morning with you sitting in the porter's quarters, looking out at the myriad mysterious lights as the Pennsy rounds the big curve at Altoona?

What is disturbing about the disappearance of the railroad train, then, isn't so much the train itself, but what it means and has meant to Americans, and to people everywhere. When we think of the Overland stage, we also think of Indians and cowboys and what the stage *meant* to the people of the Old West. When we think of the Mississippi River steamer and sidewheeler, we envision dandified slick-haired gamblers with white teeth and slippery fingers, and wide-eyed belles with beauty marks. We do the same sort of reconstruction with packets and clipper ships. We identify the times and the people with them, rather than regarding the objects for themselves. So what will it mean when the trains are gone?

It will mean the end of an era, of course; but it will also mean the end of the kind of leisure and escape that nourished men's souls for a good many years. The elegance of rail travel, along with the concomitant necessary break in routine, made one feel expansive and romantic and, for a little while, content. It was a way of life. It had *class,* the very concept of which is becoming quaint.

Airplanes are quicker and cheaper, but they offer nothing else. What is romantic about being catapulted through the air from one end of the continent to the other in five hours? What is genteel and relaxing about being strapped to a seat, or being served food in pink plastic containers? True, the sight of a city at night from 20,000 feet is enchanting, but it is not really a city you see; it is an abstract painting of lights. And your fellow passengers are abstract, for you can never really get to know them in the short time you are together. And you *are* together, because there is no such thing as privacy on a plane, except, perhaps, in the washrooms.

Contrast this aerial bus-ride with a trip on a train, assuming, always, that you are not compelled, except by your complexes, to get there in a hurry. The train is yours. You move through it like a king. Servants stand ready to do your bidding, ready to please you; just ring the bell. Your bed is made, your slightest whim catered to, your appetite is magnificent, the scenery is unsullied and just outside the window. You can have a second martini, because you are home, and a third, too, if it pleases you—the sirloin you will order can wait a bit longer. Perhaps you will have it sent in to your room, or perhaps you will prefer the diner. There's always the chance that the steward will seat you beside that remarkable blonde who seems to be traveling alone. If that is the case, you can look forward to an acquaintanceship ripening over a period of days, not hours. If you're seated, instead, beside the jolly fat man, you can always excuse yourself, return to the room, maybe take a solid whack at that Chardin book you've been trying to read, or simply retire to the crisp double-mattress bed. Next morning you can have an understanding with the steward, who will be the soul of cooperation.

What can equal this for traveling—not "getting there"—*traveling?* Should we not be sad at its passing?

No dishonest tears are shed on graveyard runs. Many stations and walks of life are represented in the common commemoration of the death of trains. These people have come to love trains, and the last trip is always a time of despair, a time for cherishing what will soon be history. Unhappily, these final one-way trips have been occurring with increasing frequency the world around.

In July 1961, ninety people on the platform of Paris's Gare de l'Est boarded the Orient Express for the last time. It is not difficult to guess the thoughts of those passengers as the great train roared across France for the final time; over the Rhine, down the Danube, the shrill whistle signaling its surrender as

it whipped past castles and cathedrals. Those people sat back
in seats that were once velvet and fringed in Brussels lace, and
they remembered other years, before the windows had begun
to rattle, before the cars had become worn and dirty; they remembered the oysters and the chilled wine served by waiters
in blue silk breeches, white stockings and buckle shoes: luxury
beyond luxury. Perhaps, also, they thought of all the mystery
stories that were written about the Express, and the characters
in those stories: the glamorous woman spy who wore mink
and nothing under it but her flesh; the one who always carried
a tiny pistol in her handbag; the smooth diplomats who were
really working for several governments at the same time; the
sturdy hero with a sardonic smile and an attaché case, full of
secret papers, locked to his wrist. And the passengers may have
wondered if the ghosts of these characters were not, in fact,
riding with them. Mostly, they were surely thinking: This is
the end. This will be no more. The Orient Express, which
made its first run June 5, 1883, will run no more.

The splendor of oldtime rail travel was not, however, confined to Europe. As far back as 1911, American trains knew
how to live. The Santa Fe De Luxe, which ran from Chicago
to Los Angeles, carried a complement of seventy persons, including a barber, a lady's maid, a manicurist and a public
secretary. It provided a library, telegraphic news reports, stock
quotations, tubs and showers, electric curling irons and stereo-
scopic views of the passing scenery along the line. The breakfast menu was more than substantial, offering such delicacies
as calf's liver sautéed, grilled French lamb chops, corned beef,
roast beef, buckwheat cakes, griddle cakes, Rocky Mountain
trout and French toast.

An antelope dinner was offered on the Overland Limited, after which passengers would be invited to raise their window sashes and take pot shots at buffalo.

All the rolling stock then was gaily varnished to a high gloss, rather like mobile country estates. The trains were immaculate, from the high-wheeled locomotives to the canopied observation platforms. There were covered bridges, water towers, hand-operated switches and bearded engineers in derby hats. The engines never wore out, even after as many as fifty years of service; and those in the know maintain that the steamers were more dependable and every bit as fast as the later Diesels. The introduction of the Diesel seems, in restrospect, to have been merely an economy move. Nonetheless, it took over, and that is when the lustre began to tarnish.

Who can forget the conductors in muttonchop whiskers and blue tailcoats, the thunder and fire that exploded from the tall stacks of Taunton-built engines with crimson-and-gold lettering on their tenders, the time when station agents' and dispatchers' offices buzzed with telegraph keys and batteries of telephones? All along the right-of-way it was freedom scented with coal smoke or wood smoke, and passengers answering the friendly waves of field-plowing farmers and barefoot children (they weren't really disdainful). Freedom in union, and in experience shared.

Fittingly, locomotives were accorded the same respect as ocean liners. They were ladies, whereas the Diesels, like airplanes, were neuter genders. Everybody loved the high iron with its proudly polished brass, not merely the railroad people but everybody. It was natural. A steam engine, panting hoarsely as she climbs a grade, or breathing sweet as she runs along an open stretch, or crying in the night, a cry of pain or joy, depending, was no thing of metal. She was alive.

She was also many. On some lines she was the girl next door; on others, a queen. In 1870 she was an empress, her drive-spokes fire-red, drive-rods silver, the iron on her boilers iridescent blue, the scrollwork on her engine cabs and running boards emblazoned with gold leaf and crimson varnish. And that was only right, for she was pulling the luxury palace cars.

Those cars reached a point of elegance undreamt of before or after. They had rosewood paneling, chandeliers of purest crystal, velvet hangings, fringes, draperies, inlaid wood in sleeping apartments, drawing rooms and connecting staterooms rich with brocades, divans with cushions and hassocks, dressing rooms, bevel-edged mirrors, and a cuisine prepared by internationally famous chefs.

Anyone at all could enjoy these cars on a cross-country jaunt, provided he could afford to rent the entire train. And in that turn-of-the-century time, when Mr. Astor made his democratic remark ("Anybody with a million dollars is as well off as if he were rich!"), no small number could do exactly that.

Less plutocratic citizens made do with the privately owned railroad car. Unknown today, the private car was at one time the dream of every American, for it was the touchstone of success, the supreme symbol of having Arrived—as opulent and luxurious as the age that created it. For fifty years these cars moved splendidly over America's rails in a wake of sighs and heartbeats. Any millionaire, socialite, industrialist, or national figure who did not own at least one had not succeeded in any real sense. But ownership was only the beginning. One had to have the best car; and this led to bitter competition. Period furniture was installed, and pipe organs, rare paintings, solid gold and silver dinner services, marble plumbing fixtures, ceiling murals, gigantic mirrors and costly upholsteries. The first air-conditioned railroad car was privately owned; it belonged to Charles Louis Fleischmann, the yeast tycoon. Mrs. J. P. Donahue's car, called the *Japauldin,* had solid-gold lighting fixtures, quartered oak beams that ran the length of the drawing-room ceiling, and a wood-burning fireplace. Ignace Paderewski had his own car, the *General Stanley,* and of course it contained a piano. American Presidents from Lincoln's time forward rode grandly on campaigns and official tours aboard private cars—but today, United States Railroad Car No. 1, the *Magellan,* is rented to the government by the Association of American Railroads for a dollar a year for the President's use. It was built during Franklin Roosevelt's time and is approximately as ornate as a stock-broker's office. Not that it matters: our Presidents travel nowadays by plane.

The private car usually included an observation drawing room that opened out onto the brass-railed open-air platform. The rest of the car consisted of several sleeping apartments, a salon for dining, accommodating eight or ten, a galley, pantry, storerooms, iceboxes and sleeping quarters for the crew.

The ultimate in private-car ownership was achieved during the time of George Jay Gould, the railroad sachem. His guests were expected to appear for dinner in full formal evening attire.

For most of the more than 350 varnished masterpieces, the end came long ago on the rip track. Jay Gould's fabulous

Atalanta, built in the eighties for $50,000, faded away as a yardmaster's shack on the Missouri Pacific in Overton, Texas. The car that hauled the Prince of Wales about the U.S. during his tour here in 1924 is the home of a coal-stripping gang in Hazleton, Pennsylvania.

Only two private cars are in use today for the pleasure and convenience of their owners: the *Helma,* home of Bruce Dodson, a Kansas City insurance magnate, and *The Gold Coast,* owned and operated by Lucius Beebe and Charles Clegg. *The Gold Coast* has two master bedrooms, a twenty-four-foot-long drawing room, crystal lighting fixtures, Venetian mirrors, antimacassars and lopped and fringed draperies which recreate the interior of Leland Stanford's *Stanford,* built in the seventies.

It was George Pullman who engineered most of the elegant palace cars, but he left a broad stroke across the canvas of railroading when he developed the folding upper berth. Perhaps his sleepers were a departure from the Victorian elegance of his previous inspirations, but they were immensely popular. By 1916 the Pullman Company operated 7,500 sleeping cars over 137 railroads; and 260,000 persons occupied those berths every year.

The next change, as noted, was the replacement of steam engines with Diesels. We even tried to engender some kind of affection for the oil eaters, giving them nicknames like chugglebugs, hinky dinks, galloping geese and bungaloos; but it wasn't the same. The punka-punk, punka-punk of the Diesel seemed too efficient, too utilitarian. It had none of the warmth and majesty of the steam engines that now had begun to gather the patina of antiquity on a thousand spurs, in roundhouses and in scrap yards. The full-speed sound it made was powerful, but contemptuous; and we bitterly missed the stirring, spiritual cry of the steamers.

And now the Diesels themselves are going, and their contempt is honorable. That of the personnel of all but a few trains is not. Aware that they are dying, the porters and conductors, the news butchers and dining-car stewards are behaving like cranky nonagenarians. They are rude, inept, surly and impatient. The best of them would have been dressed down and summarily fired in the old days. The same would happen to them today on the Twentieth Century Limited, the Broadway Limited, the Super Chief, and a half dozen others. But these men probably wouldn't care. Their pride is gone.

That is the unbearable loss to railroad men, and they know it. Our loss is greater, but we don't know it. We fancy that we have rid ourselves of an inefficient means of transportation. Instead, we have rid ourselves of one of the two remaining refuges, one of the two sanctuaries where a man can retreat from the maelstrom and become acquainted with himself.

And how will ocean liners fare when the 2,500 miles-per-hour airship is perfected?

How will Man fare?